Praise for

MASTER YOUR BUSINESS CASH FLOW™

"Just one idea in this book can make you thousands of dollars—this book contains thousands of ideas."

—Henry DeVries, co-author, *How to Close a Deal Like Warren Buffett*, and *Persuade with a Story!*

"Cash is oxygen to a business, yet most entrepreneurs mishandle that oxygen and come close to suffocation. This book is a must-read for entrepreneurs who wish to learn and understand how to manage that oxygen flow in order to successfully scale their business."

—Adam Witty, founder and CEO, Advantage Media Group author, speaker, and philanthropist

"As an entrepreneur and small-business CEO, I've learned (the hard way) that cash flow is the lifeblood of a business. In Al Zdenek' s book, *Master Your Business Cash Flow*™, he delivers simple and straightforward processes to make better business and personal financial decisions. These concrete concepts show you how to have the power to achieve what you wish and when. Specifically, Al's chapter about forming a 'Championship Team' of experts around you is right on the mark. If you want your business to reach new heights and learn how to make correct financial choices all the time, read this book."

—Dr. Tony Alessandra, author, *The Platinum Rule*, and *The NEW Art of Managing People*

"With life being so stressful and chaotic, I constantly seek solutions that are quick to understand, fast to implement, efficient, and effective. This book checks all of those boxes. It provides an easy-to-implement blueprint that virtually any business person can use. It will allow you to find more cash flow, create wealth, and simplify your business and personal life. After reading this book, I am fervent believer in *Master Your Business Cash Flow™!*"

—Rick Sapio, founder, Mutual Capital Alliance, Inc.;
USA Mutuals, Inc.; and Business Finishing School, LLC, entrepreneur

In *Master Your Business Cash Flow™*, Al provides pragmatic advice that reflects decades of solid business experience—not just with driving success, but just as importantly, how to turn failure into success. So often business books share platitudes that are hard to relate to, but Al brings his ideas back to earth so business people can turn those ideas into reality.

—Rachel Braun Scherl, managing partner and co-founder,
SPARK Solutions for Growth, author and speaker

"Actionable, pragmatic, and built from real-world experiences, *Master Your Business Cash Flow™* is a must-read for business owners looking to create a successful, enduring business. Cash flow is like oxygen for any business. With healthy cash flow, your business can grow and thrive, but without that air flowing into your business, even great products, great services, and the great people delivering them will gasp and sputter. If you had the courage to start your own business, congratulations—you have made it further than most. Now give it the life it deserves by mastering your cash flow."

—Dave Welling, CEO, Mercer Advisors

"I wish I would have read *Master Your Business Cash Flow*™ when I was running a business. I thought that it was all about sales and profit. But every company only goes out of business for one reason—cash flow! This book has practical and easy ways to find more cash flow and accelerate your wealth!"

—Barry Moltz, author, *Small Business Hacks: 100 Shortcuts to Success*, host, Business Insanity Talk Radio, small business expert

"With so many financial books to pick from, how does one pick the right book to grow one's business? I started a new business six years ago and there was no bible like this. After reading *Master Your Business Cash Flow*™, I highly recommend this as a must-read for all business executives, no matter what size or stage their company is in. The chapter which really hits home to me was 'Create a Championship Team of Experts.' Al Zdenek hits the nail on the head, as the right team with exemplary qualities is the key to a prosperous business and a good working environment."

—Pam Laudenslager, chairperson and CEO, Center Stage Capital, Inc., two-time Tony-award-winning Broadway producer

"*Master Your Business Cash Flow*™ not only has great financial knowledge to share, but Al makes it more poignant with relevant personal experience about *not* mastering his cash flow. You can tell Al has a deep understanding and empathy for people in similar circumstances. I especially recommend that my fellow entrepreneurs and business leaders read Al's book and apply its principles."

—Corey Kupfer, president, Authentic Enterprises, LLC; and Authentic Business Academy, expert strategist, dealmaker, business consultant, and entrepreneur

"*Master Your Business Cash Flow*™ is the bible that all business people and entrepreneurs need to read. My first business venture went under. I had no cash reserves to keep us afloat until the income came in. I knew the medical industry well but not basic financial principles. Reading this book, I now have the most important piece of the puzzle: mastering cash flow, making the best financial choices all of the time, and being an effective CEO."

—R.F. Ledon, MD, bestselling author, businessman, and entrepreneur

"What makes *Master Your Business Cash Flow*™ such a great book is its passion and mission to ensure you live the life you want now and in the future and always make the 100 percent correct financial decision. This book is as just as compassionate about your life as it is passionate about finance. Al Zdenek explains financial principles and techniques in plain, everyday language so everyone can understand and grow. I've learned more from this book than I've learned from all finance books I've read. This book demystifies wealth building and makes me feel like I can do it, too!"

—Carla Moore, vice president of sales strategy, HBO

"The worst part about owning a business is waking up to the fear and anxiety that unforeseen circumstances from your choices are going to bankrupt your dreams. I've seen over one hundred different entrepreneurs with one hundred different 'strategies' all hit that point. Al Zdenek lays out a fundamental roadmap to the key driver of sound sleep: Mastering Your Cash Flow. His authentic and vulnerable approach gets you out of your head and into a plan that sets specific cash flow goals for yourself and your business. This book is now required reading for every business owner in my portfolio.

—Jamie McIntyre, founder and CEO, Rewire Capital, entrepreneur

"In *Master Your Business Cash Flow*™, Al Zdenek brings real-life perspective as a business owner, a CPA, and a personal financial planner to the choices people make on their way to success or failure. What many business owners fail to appreciate in their business is the one asset over which they have direct control as an investment. As a result, they use it as an ATM to buy things rather than as an engine to drive things. Al's wisdom and insight, gleaned from many years advising others as well as living through his own choices, makes this book a helpful guide in the road to financial independence."

—Mark Tibergien, CEO, Pershing Advisor Solutions

"Would you take business advice from a CPA—a *smart* CPA—who ran his first business into the ground? Well you *should!* Al Zdenek has written the most honest business book I've ever read (and I've read, at last count, 379 of them over my forty-one years in business). I've wasted a lot of time reading books by oh-so-successful businesspeople who paint a rosy and boastful picture of their brilliant careers. *Master Your Business Cash Flow*™ is full of great insights, great advice, and great honesty."

—Greg Godek, author, *1001 Ways to be Romantic*, and *How to be Mildly Brilliant*

"Al Zdenek proves that lightening can strike twice—*Master Your Business Cash Flow*™, is the second excellent book in the *Master Your Cash Flow* series. This latest work is full of wisdom, invaluable lessons, and, most of all, expert guidance, especially for readers with a growing business for whom effective cash flow is absolutely critical. As CEO of an expanding nonprofit organization with nearly one hundred employees, mastering Al's principles have been never been more important to me."

—D. Brenton Simons, president and CEO,
New England Historic Genealogical Society

"Reading *Master Your Business Cash Flow*™ was powerful confirmation that what we have to do is keep ourselves on the right track and we have to make the best financial decisions. Each chapter presents a powerful truth. It was good to read about the proper lessons to use in wealth planning. My life was completely changed with these teachings. It got me going in the right direction. Life is good."

—Dave Hainsworth, CPA, CFP, president, David N. Hainsworth, CPA, PC

"I'm on a mission to change the world for the better—but no *money*, no *mission*. Like many entrepreneurs, I'd reached a point where I was no longer running the business—the business was running me (a miserable form of exercise, to say the least!). Cash flow would become cash stop. Thanks to Al Zdenek's Wealth Building Formula®, I'm finally able to master my cash flow and do the work I'm called to do."

—Karyn Buxman, neurohumorist,
author, *Funny Means Money: Strategic Humor for Influence*

"If there's one lesson I've learned as the founder and CEO of an investment bank that advises clients on liquidity events, it's that cash is king. *Master Your Business Cash Flow*™ is a must-read with real-world examples of enhancing the cash flows and value of any business."

—Elizabeth Bloomer Nesvold, founder and CEO, Silver Lane Advisors,
author, *Art of M&A: Valuation*

"Al's storytelling in *Master Your Business Cash Flow*™ made me feel in a real and raw way how critical cash flow planning and decision making is to both the short- and long-term health of businesses. His straightforward teachings help create actionable steps to manage your business and find more of that critical cash."

—Richard Cancro, founder and CEO, AdvisorEngine

"*Master Your Business Cash Flow*™ has completely altered my so-called business plan. Juggling too much, buried in work, and not taking enough time to work on the business is perhaps my biggest revelation. I love Al Zdenek's practical and easy ways to find more cash flow to help me quickly grow the value of not only my business but my overall wealth. If you want to transform your business and your life, read this book now."

—Kate Delaney, business motivational speaker, consultant, author, syndicated talk show host

MASTER YOUR BUSINESS CASH FLOW™

MASTER YOUR BUSINESS CASH FLOW™

GROW THE COMPANY YOU LOVE, LIVE THE LIFE YOU WANT NOW

ALBERT J. ZDENEK, JR., CPA/PFS

ForbesBooks

Published by ForbesBooks, Charleston, South Carolina.
Member of Advantage Media Group.

ForbesBooks is a registered trademark, and the ForbesBooks colophon is a trademark of Forbes Media, LLC.

Printed in the United States of America.

10 9 8 7 6 5 4 3 2 1

ISBN: 978-1-946633-21-7
LCCN: 2018955612

Cover design by Carly Blake.
Layout design by Megan Elger.

This publication is designed to provide accurate and authoritative information in regard to the subject matter covered. It is sold with the understanding that the publisher is not engaged in rendering legal, accounting, or other professional services. If legal advice or other expert assistance is required, the services of a competent professional person should be sought.

Advantage Media Group is proud to be a part of the Tree Neutral® program. Tree Neutral offsets the number of trees consumed in the production and printing of this book by taking proactive steps such as planting trees in direct proportion to the number of trees used to print books. To learn more about Tree Neutral, please visit **www.treeneutral.com**.

Since 1917, the Forbes mission has remained constant. Global Champions of Entrepreneurial Capitalism. ForbesBooks exists to further that aim by bringing the Stories, Passion, and Knowledge of top thought leaders to the forefront. ForbesBooks brings you The Best in Business. To be considered for publication, please visit **www.forbesbooks.com**.

*To Alain Briscadieu-Farjas, my husband,
and to Marguerite B. Zdenek, my former wife—two people
who love me unconditionally and who have made my success
and extraordinary journey in life possible.*

Table of Contents

Acknowledgments

Success in business, careers, and as a person is the result of the generous, honest, caring, and talented guidance by many. I have been fortunate enough to have many that have contributed so much to me and in turn have inspired me to contribute to others. Those on this list made this book and the extraordinary life I lead possible. I am sure I have left some off, but not intentionally.

My deepest appreciation and gratitude begins with my wealth management mentor, Darrell W. Cain, CPA. Darrell generously gave me, a financially struggling CPA, the gift of how to recover financially, become financially independent in the time frame I wanted, and he inspired me to change my career and go on to be a contribution to anyone I could. He allowed me to see that I could empower people to live the life they want now and in the future. I have achieved what I have in the wealth management profession due to him.

Sharon Tiger, EdD, is more than a life coach. She taught me that wealth management is more than money; it is also ensuring your team, clients, family, and friends lived a fulfilled and loving life. Dr. David Zelman taught me unconditional love and how to live the life you want. I live the extraordinary life I do today because of Darrell, Sharon, and David.

While this book is the culmination of a fun and exciting life journey, there are many others that made my journey and this book possible. Many thanks to the Advantage Media Group|ForbesBooks team of Jenny Tripp, Eland Mann, Saara Khalil, and Arthur McKey. Others that made this book and my extraordinary life possible include my parents, Albert J. Zdenek, Sr. and Rose Marie Prince; my grandmother, Marie Rose Prince; and many others including Rose Marie Zdenek Brown; James D. Zdenek; Joseph E.L. Zdenek; Albert J. Zdenek III; Marie Rose Ancone; Joe and Marie Laggini; Bob Laggini; Chris Laggini; Stephanie Laggini Fiore; Teresa Laggini Sankner; Bernard V. Switzer; Frank Caterini; Miss Delli Paoli; Dr. Scott Whitener; Stephen E. Scebelo, CPA; Arthur Eckerson, Jr.; Frank Bonner; Joe Mazzotta; Johnny Love; Karen Dare; Charles Kuski; Susanne Kuski; Rich and Christine DeFrehn; Ed Coleman; Dorothy Latimer; Bob Latimer; Bob Klein, CPA; Rich Encherra; Henry and Grace Koster; Pat Moran; Peter Arnold; John Sweetman; Greg Campbell; Ed Hogan; Ruth Claus; Glenn Woo; Larry Rappaport; Kirby Fowler; Gretchen Craig; Bill Hengen; Bill and Ginger Koster; Charley and Monica Accurso; Patti and George Sousa; Frank and Patty Granato; Bruce Raiffe; Paul and Ruth Woolard; Mark Tibergien; Tony Riotto; Andy Putterman; Paul Lally; Rich Cancro; Jamie McIntyre; Brian Picariello; Rick Weyers; John Silletto; Barry Newman, CPA; Bryan Bielawski, CPA; D. Brenton Simons; Henry DeVries; Michael Hauge; Tony Alessandra; Liz Bloomer Nesvold;

Rachel Braun Scherl; Adam Witty; Deborah Ridgill; Rick Sapio; Damon Gersh; Dave Welling; Barry Moltz; Pam Laudenslager; Corey Kupfer; Ray Fernandez-Ledon; Carla Moore; Karyn Buxman; Greg Godek; Kate Delaney; Rusty Shelton; Dave Hainesworth, CPA; John F. Furth; Daniel Chartock; Dean Minuto; and Betty Ng.

While I am sure I have missed some, this list would not be complete without my former wife and one of the best friends I have in the world, Marguerite (Margie) B. Laggini Zdenek, and my soulmate and *partenaire pour toujours*, my husband, Alain Briscadieu-Farjas, to both of whom this book is dedicated.

About the Author

For over thirty years, Al Zdenek has empowered thousands of people to transform their lives by educating them to make better financial decisions that allow them to live the life they want now and for the rest of their lives. He is executive vice president of Mercer Advisors, the highly regarded wealth management firm headquartered in Santa Barbara, California. Before joining Mercer, Al founded and was the president and CEO of Traust Sollus Wealth Advisors, NYC.

As a nationally recognized bestselling author, speaker, and wealth advisor, he previously authored *Master Your Cash Flow: The Key to Grow And Retain Wealth*. Al has consulted and given speeches and workshops to thousands of business owners, entrepreneurs, C-suite executives, and individuals who have transformed their lives by applying the education and proprietary processes he created. Knowing how to make better financial decisions will allow one to make the 100 percent correct financial decision all the time.

Al has been selected to appear in many of the nation's top financial advisors lists and is often quoted in the media about wealth building and wealth management topics. He is often asked to present on wealth management and is a prominent keynote speaker at conferences around the country. He is a graduate from Rutgers College and from Rutgers Graduate School of Business. He lives in Manhattan and Paris.

Foreword

IS YOUR BUSINESS GIVING YOU THE LIFE YOU WANT?

By Dr. David Zelman

Are you living the life you want *now*, or just hoping you'll be able to have it when you retire?

Are you mastering your cash flow, or just praying it will increase?

Are you using debt strategically, or are you simply *in* debt?

Do you know with certainty that you're reducing your taxes in a way that will allow your business to grow and thrive?

And is your business leading you to independent wealth and the freedom to do what you want, when you want?

Imagine if you could reduce your financial anxiety, frustration, and stress, find additional cash flow to grow your business, live the life you want now, and achieve your goals—and financial freedom—quicker than you dreamed.

With the help of this book, you can. I know, because that is what Al Zdenek has done for me. I have been his client for almost twenty years, and in that time he has transformed my business and my life.

In 2000 I owned a stock called My Points. It was trading at $104 a share, and at that price I had a net worth of almost $2 million. For the first time in my life, I was experiencing a sense of freedom around money. I was in control of my destiny. It was an incredible feeling.

Then, in 2001, it all disappeared.

With the crash, I lost over 60 percent of my investments. I had to sell off the My Points holdings for fifteen dollars a share—in other words, for around fifteen cents for every dollar I'd invested.

Everything else started collapsing as well. I'm the founder and CEO of Transitions Institute, a consulting company that focuses on leadership and high performance. Business was depressed everywhere, and our month-to-month revenue fell to the point where I had to let some of my employees go.

And as my business took a downward spiral, so did those feelings of financial freedom and control over my future. I was at a loss for how to turn things around, so my wife Karen and I began meeting with financial planners. None of them gave us any hope for the future—until we started working with Al Zdenek.

When we first entered Al's office, we had little hope his advice would be any different. We expected to hear what we'd heard from everyone else: "You're just fifteen years away from retirement, then you'll need $4 to $5 million to live comfortably. So you'll need to put away $250,000 away each year."

I kept wanting to say, "If we had $250,000 to put away, we wouldn't be here talking to you." But instead we'd just move on to the next advisors who would tell us pretty much the same thing.

But Al was different. His knowledge and mastery of finance immediately gave us hope.

He began by asking us what we wanted our lives to be, now and in the future. Then he presented us with his Master Your Cash Flow™ process, along with his Wealth Building Formula® process. These gave us a model and a structure for the next steps we'd take—a pathway to recovering and securing our financial freedom (the same magical secrets you'll find in this book).

Then Al helped establish a Defined Benefit pension plan for me so I could achieve a far greater tax deferment each year than I had with my 401(k). It would also allow us to save enough create a financially free retirement and to create a surplus to leave to our children.

But I still had to generate enough revenue and income to support these plans. Al laid out his brilliant ideas for transforming my cash flow issues. He encouraged me to *raise* my fees—by 100 percent!—rather than to lower them as I had planned. And to my surprise, almost no one balked at the increase, and I had no reduction in client flow.

Al continued working with me to master the Money Game, and to grow my business by increasing our cash reserves, by creating multiple income streams, raising capital more effectively, investing wisely, planning better, becoming more prepared and decisive, and focusing on all the other powerful tools you'll experience in this book.

Thanks to Al, Karen and I have that incredible feeling of freedom and financial independence back. We have a real sense of control over how the future will unfold. We have referred many friends, family, and clients to Al, and without exception, they have expressed their deepest gratitude for bringing him into their lives.

And I feel happy and privileged to now do the same for you.

When you read *Master Your Business Cash Flow™: Grow the Company You Love, Live the Life You Want Now*, and follow Al's wisdom, you'll see your own business and cash flow grow. Your dreams of financial freedom and independence will become real, and your peace of mind will return. Your life will be transformed.

Enjoy the journey.

Dr. David Zelman,
Founder and CEO, Transitions Institute

Introduction

I was sitting in my office at 12 Minneakoning Road, Flemington, New Jersey. It had come to this; I had no choice. I had to let go one-third of my staff—eight of twenty-four people immediately. I couldn't make the next payroll. I quickly called them all into a room, and told them they no longer worked with the firm.

"Go back to your desks, pack up, hand in your keys, and leave."

They had not seen this coming. Their stunned, shocked faces—some crying—haunt me to this day. My company had become one of the most successful CPA firms in Hunterdon County in just five years. Now we were going under.

I lived in a well-known Victorian house on a prominent corner in town whose magnificent four-story tower was a familiar landmark in Flemington. I was on the borough council and the police commission. Everyone knew where we lived; they knew we had spent a lot of money and years restoring this famous house to its former glory.

A few days before, I'd sat my wife Margie down in the parlor of this beautiful home that she had so lovingly restored and raised our two sons within to tell her, "I don't know if, at the end of all this, we'll be able to keep the house."

She started crying. But then—to her everlasting credit—she resolutely wiped her eyes and said, "Okay, what do we have to do?"

Poor business and personal financial decisions had caught up with me. I was now on the verge of bankruptcy and financial ruin. How could this have happened? I was a CPA!

Some experiences in life leave an indelible imprint on us, and forever alter the way in which we view the world. These were among those experiences, and certainly among the worst, in my life.

Months before, my operations manager, Ruth, told me, "Al, if we do not take action soon, whether it's getting more cash in the door or cutting expenses, we won't be able to make payroll someday in the very near future." That would be the death knell for my company. But I ignored the danger signs. I told myself we could work our way out of this. Something would happen to save us. Being more realistic, Ruth added, "I've drawn up a list of the whole team and their importance to the company, in priority order. That way we know who to release first when the time comes." She had put herself first on that list. Eventually she joined the others that were called into the conference room, where I bluntly dismissed them. My actions, or in this case, my inaction, had caused this—the loss of jobs and security for my team, the probable loss of my family's home. I swore that when I got by this, I would never let it happen again.

My back to the wall, I finally started to take action. I was now out to survive. Margie had been there when I started the business, doing administrative work, so I drafted her to be my office manager—of course, with no pay. Her new job included fielding calls from angry vendors wanting payment. We couldn't pay them, so we started cutting deals with them: "Look, we can't pay you for six months.

If you give us that time and keep supporting us now, we'll pay you everything. If you don't agree with that, we'll just cut you off and we'll get another vendor." Most agreed, but some could not. We found other vendors to keep us going.

I was constantly being served with papers for lawsuits. I got used to our receptionist calling me to the front desk saying, "Al, we have the sheriff's office here again." And all through it, I had to keep up the enthusiasm of my team and let them know everything was going to be all right, though there were many days I was not sure. With all of this on my mind, I had to run the company and go out and find business to bring us back from the edge.

As an employer, as the CEO of a business, I had tremendous responsibility for my employees, and I let them down. I made poor business financial choices, and did not run the enterprise well. Yes, I paid for it. But in the process I made eight other people along with their families pay for my mistakes, and that's a burden of guilt that still weighs on me all these years later.

Only later on would I understand I was playing what I call "The Money Game" badly. Part of the game is managing your cash flow well: being a master of your cash flow and making the right financial decisions, the right moves. I had not, and I was paying for it.

So, what is the Money Game, anyway? Similar to checkers, chess, or any other type of game:

- there are rules to follow,

- there are good moves and bad moves,

- the point is to win,

- make poor moves and you lose, and

- the better you understand the rules and know how to make the right moves, the more you will win—maybe even become a master at it.

But there's a lot more at stake in the Money Game than in a typical checkers game: if you play it poorly, your business may go under. You may need to work more years in life, harder than necessary, and still might not achieve the wealth you need to live the life you want for yourself, so it's a game you want to get really good at. We will talk more about that later.

There's a lot more at stake in the Money Game than in a typical checkers game: if you play it poorly, your business may go under.

I learned some critical lessons and some key moves of the Money Game that subsequently helped my firm and me through the crash of 2008 some twenty years later: I learned that I needed to have cash reserves, because I couldn't depend on banks. I learned, too, that I couldn't depend on just one stream of income, but needed to have multiple streams so that when unexpected reverses like this occurred we'd be impacted but not devastated. And I learned to be an effective CEO, to take corrective action immediately—because, like so many inexperienced business owners, I kept expecting things would somehow turn around. They didn't. Those changes in how I did business meant that when the crash of 2008 came, I didn't have to lay anyone off. Yes, we had to tighten our belts (cut all unnecessary expenses, stop bonuses, and temporarily suspend our 401(k) plan contribution), but we kept the whole staff. As bad as that experience was in the 1980s, it made a better CEO out of me. I had learned how to run a business well.

WHAT KILLS A BUSINESS?

According to the Bureau of Labor Statistics, only 50 percent of small businesses will survive five years or more. Approximately one-third will survive ten years or more.[1] These bald statistics don't begin to express the human suffering those failures leave behind.

What fatal errors do entrepreneurs and CEOs make that contribute to this high rate of failure? Often they're tied to how we look at our businesses, and our places in them:

- **Playing House.** When I was a little kid, my older sister, the neighbor girl, and I played house. Most of the time I was cast as the baby, but we'd switch around, all acting just like the grown-ups we knew (at least, our best imitations of them). Sounds like a silly kids' game, but this is just how I've seen many business owners act: It's not real for them. They are in a fantasy world. They don't know how to make the best financial decisions. They don't want to make hard decisions, nor do they know *how*. They haven't planned the business properly, so they might as well be kids pretending to be in charge.

- **"Field of Dreams" / "If you build it, they will come."** Jamie McIntyre, founder and CEO of Rewire Capital, warns, "You have to have sales to start a business, you need solid margin to sustain a business, and you need cash flow to grow the business. I have never seen a 'Field of Dreams' business model work."[2] To an excited and passionate

---

1   Bureau of Labor Statistics, "Entrepreneurship and the US Economy: Chart 3, Survival Rates of Establishments, by Year Started and Number of Years Since Starting, 1994–2015, in percent," Last modified April 28, 2016, https://www.bls.gov/bdm/entrepreneurship/bdm_chart3.htm.

2   Jamie McIntyre, interview with author.

business owner it seems logical. Of course, everyone's going to want what they're selling, because it's so great. They don't realize how difficult it is to create that funnel of customers. They assume it's just as simple as opening the doors. Is being a parent simple? No. Is the tax code simple? No, and neither is establishing and running a successful business.

Entrepreneurs, generally optimistic and creative, take undue risks more often than an ordinary business person would. They do best when partnered with someone who takes a more pragmatic approach in planning the business and amassing reserves. Those stories you read about successful people who gambled everything and started their business on their credit card are inspiring. But the stories you don't hear are the ones in which those people gambled everything they had and lost, because they don't make such great copy. Trust me, they're far more common.

But there are other more basic causes, too. Lack of financial literacy is a major stumbling block for many. A survey of Americans over the age of fifty that asked three basic questions about compound interest, inflation, and risk diversification found that only a third of respondents answered all three questions correctly.[3]

There is also a lack of financial comprehension and understanding of human financial behavior. In other words, most people know the name of the game but don't understand how to play it well.

It is like playing chess: you may know what a king, bishop, or pawn looks like, but can you move them strategically? The difference in financial literacy and comprehension is the same.

---

3   Annamaria Lusardi, and Olivia S. Mitchell, "Financial Literacy and Planning: Implications for Retirement Wellbeing," National Bureau of Economic Research, working paper no. 17078, May 2011, http://www.nber.org/papers/w17078.

You may know the principle "compounding," but can you apply it correctly in making the best financial decision? The great majority cannot. You may know how to take out a loan or mortgage, but can you choose the right one that builds wealth the most for you? The great majority cannot. You can understand some terms of the new tax law, but can you take advantage of it in the best way possible? Yes, I know, you leave that up to your CPA. But most CPAs do not know how to apply comprehension either. I know—I was one of them.

So, how much does emotion play into your decisions rather than the actual calculations? Very often, it's what financial decisions are based on.

Understanding literacy and comprehension allows you to make sound financial moves and to avoid poor or even disastrous ones. But most play this game poorly.

As a young man starting out in the '80s, I had youthful optimism and a good skill set as an experienced CPA. I had financial literacy, but I lacked financial comprehension. Most successful business owners, professionals, and CEOs are like this. They know how to make money but have trouble keeping it. On top of this, like many entrepreneurs who chase every opportunity like a squirrel chasing acorns, I got involved in too many ventures outside of my area of expertise and consequently spread myself too thin.

My mission now (and the reason I'm writing this book) is to help you—whether you're the small- or medium-sized business owner, the entrepreneur starting out, or the person tasked with running the company—avoid the pitfalls I hit, and to empower you to run your business in a way that will allow you to live the life you want now and in the future.

One thing I know: all businesses operate on the same set of principles. I don't care whether it's a medical practice, Amazon, your local grocery store, or your accountant. They all operate the same way, and they either succeed or fail because of the similar financial choices they make. If you're clear on how to make the best financial choices, you're likely to be among the happy 50 percent that succeed.

How did I survive? I made it through via a combination of determination and luck. I put my pride aside and asked for help. I found a wonderful mentor who taught me to play the Money Game along with many other financial lessons I'm going to teach you here. The advice I got, and the championship team of professionals I eventually assembled, helped me become the success I am today. I am truly living the life I want. I travel the world; I have homes in the US and in Paris. I, along with the many people I have helped, am living proof that my principles work—and they can work for you.

Whether you're starting a business, managing a business, dreaming of opening a business, or are already in business but looking for more success, this book will help you:

- plan your business better;

- make the best business financial decisions all of the time;

- create or change the way your business operates so it can help you to live the life you want now, and to achieve financial independence in the time frame you want or sooner;

- reduce business-related anxiety, frustration, and stress; and

- find more cash flow and higher valuation for the business.

But before we begin this journey, let's cover the ground rules of how we will work together so that you can get the most out of it.

THE GROUND RULES FOR SUCCESS

I. THIS BOOK IS NOT GOING TO ANSWER ALL YOUR QUESTIONS.

Rather, this book is meant to give you the impetus to start asking them. It's meant to guide you and educate you. I can recommend a course of action, but ultimately, you make all the decisions. No one is going to do this for you. This is your business, your life, your money, and no one is going to have more interest in these areas than you.

To succeed in getting where you want to go, you'll need to create a personal financial plan for yourself and then a plan for the business. Your personal financial plan—your personal and customized Wealth Building Formula® (discussed in a later chapter)—will serve as the starting point of your action plan aimed toward achieving your business goals and your personal financial goals. Like a well-run business comparing its current year to the previous one, it will be a reference point from which you'll be able to review your progress each year and ensure that you are on the right track to achieving your personal financial-planning goals via your business.

2. THIS IS *YOUR* BUSINESS AND PERSONAL FINANCIAL PLAN, AND YOU MUST PARTICIPATE IN IT.

Yes, you will need an expert team, but no team and no advisor can make your financial decisions for you. This must be your business and personal plan, because these are your goals, and they affect how you live now and in your future. Don't hand the reins to anyone.

Your personal Wealth Building Formula® and road map will serve as guides in letting you know exactly where you are on this journey. The journey may seem to go slowly at first, but keep in mind that this is a marathon, not a sprint. Pay attention, ask questions, and take an active role.

3. PAST DECISIONS—LET THEM GO

People come to us having made some excellent financial decisions, and some come to us having made poor financial decisions. I understand that you might feel some regret and embarrassment over past mistakes, but we're not here to belabor them or to place blame, and we're not going to shame you. This book is here to help you make better financial choices going forward that are aligned with your personal financial and lifestyle goals. We can't change the past, but we can learn from it.

WHAT ARE THE RESPONSIBILITIES OF THIS BOOK?

To answer as many of the potential questions you may have, as clearly as I can, to give you a process for making better financial choices, better clarity regarding concepts like making cash-flow management decisions, and to inspire you to achieve the financial life you wish to lead now and in the future.

CHAPTER ONE

PLAN YOUR BUSINESS FOR HOW YOU WANT TO LIVE NOW AND IN THE FUTURE

"If you can dream it, you can do it"
—**Walt Disney**

J erry, the CEO of a business services company, contacted me when it was nearly too late to save the company he'd helped found. He didn't own all the shares, and had to report to the board, so he was effectively an employee. The business was established in early 2000, and had gotten off to a strong start, quickly picking up a lot of executive clients who were eager to use their high-end services. But when the market crashed later in that year, the first thing to go was executive perks, and his company suddenly found itself on the ropes.

He'd called his board together and told them, "We have a negative cash flow of about $50,000 a month, and reserves to get us through the next six months. But if we don't come up with something soon, we're going under." The board had a lot of suggestions—all of which he'd already tried. None of them had been in this position before and they were out of ideas, so he came to me.

He told me they'd invested in a lot of expensive software, computer hardware, and other equipment, and they were making lease payments of $900,000 a year, or $75,000 per month.

I suggested, "The first thing I would do is go to your leasing company, tell them you can't pay this much, and renegotiate your terms."

"I already tried that. They said no."

"Then stop paying them," I said. "I guarantee they'll get right on the phone with you once they don't receive their payment. They may even allow two or three payments to pass, and threaten to start legal action. But if you tell them that you're not going to pay them anymore unless they renegotiate, I promise you they will. We're in a recession now. If you offer to keep on paying but at a reduced rate under different terms, you're going to rise to the top because other customers have probably stopped paying altogether." At first the idea made him uncomfortable. He took pride in always paying his obligations in a timely manner. But he saw it was his only option, and as the CEO of the company his duty to protect existence of the business, the shareholders, and the employees in any way he could.

I continued, "You should also call your landlord and inform them of your cash flow issue. Let them know, 'I can't pay your full rent right now. I do intend to fulfill the lease obligation and if you give me time and better terms temporarily, I'll pay every cent of the original lease.' Tell your leasing companies too that you'll pay every cent owed over time but you can't do it now."

In addition, I suggested he could also tell the vendors to whom he owed the most that he was not going to pay them fully for at least three to six months, but would continue services, with the warning, "If you don't continue my services, I'll just get another vendor. But if you work with me, I will make sure you are paid every cent."

He followed my advice, and was shocked at how quickly these companies came to terms with him. Now the company found cash flow of $70,000 a month more than offsetting the negative cash flow of $50,000 per month. They weren't making a profit, but they'd reduced their negative cash flow to where they were seeing positive cash flow. When the recession ended, they made good on all of their obligations and more importantly, saved the business, the employee's jobs, and the investment of the owners. They ended up doing extremely well.

WHY DO PEOPLE START BUSINESSES?

According to a November 22, 2017, *New York Times* article, 99.7 percent of all businesses have fewer then five hundred employees (80 percent of these or more than 23 million businesses are one-person-enterprises).[4] There are a lot of reasons people take the plunge—and the risks—of starting a new business. Among the reasons most often mentioned are:

---

4   Tiffany Hsu, "FCC Plan to Roll Back Net Neutrality Worries Small Businesses," *New York Times*, November 21, 2017, https://www.nytimes.com/2017/11/22/business/net-neutrality-small-businesses.html?login=email&auth=login-email.

- **Opportunity:** Americans have always had an entrepreneurial streak—the first settlers, the pioneers, were all looking for new horizons, chasing their dreams.

- **Profit:** Business founders expect to reap greater profits for their efforts than they could make working for someone else.

- **Independence:** Having a business allows you to make your own decisions and carve out your own destiny. Entrepreneur Rick Sapio lists one of his reasons as, "I love getting involved in unique opportunities without the constraint of the bureaucracy associated with working at a larger company."[5]

- **Challenge:** I started my firm December 1, 1982. Every stapler, every pencil, every computer and piece of furniture, I chose. Today I employ twenty-five people in two offices, and have clients in twenty states. That accomplishment gives me a great deal of satisfaction and pride. Every successful business owner enjoys that same pride, whether the enterprise is a newsstand or a billion-dollar business. When you build it, it's your baby.

- **Love:** Simon Sinek put his finger on the importance of this with his book, *Start with Why.* Passion for your work is the reward you get when you love what you're doing. Warren Buffett expressed it beautifully when he said he "tap-dances into work every morning." [6]

---

5   "Interview with Rick Sapio, CEO of Mutual Capital Alliance, Inc.," interview by Doug Smith, L3 Leadership, video, 54:31, April 13, 2017, https://www.youtube.com/watch?v=xfh5E1vPyls.

6   Carol Loomis, *Tap Dancing to Work: Warren Buffett on Practically Everything, 1966-2013: A Fortune Magazine Book.* (London: Portfolio Penguin, 2014).

Of course, whatever the reason you start your business, none of the above guarantees you'll find success—and certainly not every business is a pleasure to work in. But if you're passionate about your business, and if it is aligned with the life you wish to live now and in the future, you are very likely to succeed in your business venture. Conversely, even if you are making great money, if your dreams and desires aren't in alignment with your work, you won't be happy. A CPA I know makes about $700,000 a year in her own business—but she's not happy, because her dream had been to become a social worker. She actually thought of just locking the door on her office and walking away.

But regardless of whether you love your business or are merely marking time until you can unload it, the way you choose to run your business and the resulting cash flow are going to determine the way you live now, and may determine the way you live or retire in the future. Even if you're in a business now that you want to get out of, there are steps you can and should take to get it to its highest value so that you can sell it and start something closer to your heart and interests.

SUCCESS STARTS WITH A PLAN.

If your business is having problems, or if you're in a business that you're not satisfied with, how do you plan the business? Start by getting clear about what you want out of your business for your life. You have to have a comprehensive personal financial plan. You don't want to have a business that's forcing you in a direction that you don't want to go in life just because that's where the business leads you. You want to be able to dictate the business's life, not the other way around, and the only way you can do that is to know clearly what you want and need personally.

The great majority of business owners do not know what they need in terms of personal wealth. They usually have a good idea about the cash flow they need to cover their bills, but they don't have a grasp of the bigger picture—what's required to live the lifestyle they want, pay their income taxes, and build the wealth they need.

After my business went through the near-death experience I described earlier, all I could think about was survival. I wasn't just an owner; I was the managing partner and the head salesman. I was responsible for the jobs and immediate futures of some sixteen team members and their families. I had charge of the investment that two other partners made in the company. There were clients who had invested time and money in our services. They depended on us.

I wanted to make up for the income we'd lost, but I didn't have anything close to a plan. Financial planning seemed to be a new service we could offer. To me, at the time, it was just a quick fix to the business to bring in needed revenue. In the midst of all this, I sat down with a very successful financial planner and asked, "I want to know all about financial planning. I want to know how to do it, deliver it, raise revenue from it." Initially, I did not care what it could provide for *me*.

He promised that he would teach me what I'd asked, but that first I had to create my own personal financial plan: "You have to sit down and figure out what *your* financial plan is first. You have to experience the emotions that people feel when they share their most personal wants and needs around money. If you do that, I'll show you how I do everything."

I knew I was in bad shape, but until I sat down with him and put together a plan, I hadn't realized just how bad it was. As a CPA, how had I let that happen? Was I going to be able to retire some day? Am I going to be able to put my kids through college? It made me feel anxious, depressed, and stressed about the future.

When I said as much to my advisor, he replied, "Now you know how people that come to you feel. These are very intelligent people but a lot of them are having financial problems and they think they should be smart enough to handle it. They feel embarrassed. They feel humiliated. They have fears. They've got to tell you personal things they would tell no one else.

"Now, let's figure out how to get you out of this hole," he said. And he began showing me ways to increase cash flow that had never occurred to me, even though I was a great tax CPA.

That knowledge changed my whole life. I realized that this was the area of my profession that I wanted to focus on: helping other people to plan better than I had, so they could live the lifestyle they wanted now and in the future. I saw that if I did things according to the plan, I could be financially independent by the time I was fifty, which was a revelation for me. I had always thought you had to work at least to sixty-five, and then if you did not have enough, keep on working.

It stunned and excited me, and I thought to myself, "Wow, if I can share this with other people, how great would that be?" I stuck with that plan, and I was financially independent at forty-eight. Since then, I've taken many people who were in dire shape or who just needed to get on the right track to getting or maintaining true financial independence.

This changed my life and it will change yours. But it always begins with a personal financial plan. How you wish to live now and in the future will determine the plan for your business.

HOW MUCH CASH FLOW DO YOU NEED, AND WHERE CAN YOU GET IT?

I had a vision for how I wanted to live and I wasn't living that way, so I started making better decisions to increase my cash flow. I began by setting a goal: if I required X amount of dollars per year, that meant my company had to produce X amount of dollars so I could live the lifestyle I wanted to. The next question was how much cash I needed to put away so that I could be financially independent by the time I was fifty. Last, but not least, I'd need to cover my income taxes.

This isn't magic; calculating numbers is an exact science. You can calculate everything down to the penny, and if you do it correctly and build your business well enough, you can see where and when you have to pivot going forward to produce the necessary cash flow. But so many people neglect to think this through at the beginning of their business, or when they need to pivot in the direction of the business, or even make a rudimentary business plan to get them where they want to go.

Say you just wake up one day and decide to start a business— a chain of retail cosmetics stores. You could simply find an empty storefront, sign a lease, and then open the next day. But is this wise? Try to think of this beginning as the start of a road trip: I'm in New York and I want to get to San Diego. I'm eager to get on the road, so I grab my keys, hop into the car, and just start driving. I know San Diego's on the West Coast, and south of where I am, so I head in that direction. In all probability, I'll get there eventually, though it will certainly require a lot of course corrections along the way. But where and when will I stop to rest? Where will I get gas? What if my car breaks down?

In contrast, what if I were to use my phone's mapping app to route my trip? From New York to San Diego is three thousand miles. I could do about two hundred miles a day, or three hundred, or five hundred. I'll stop the first time in Harrisburg, and shave a few miles off the trip. Suddenly the whole route is laid out for me. I won't be wasting money and time taking wrong turns. I'll have more fun, and be less stressed and anxious, because I'll have less to worry about. My trip is planned, and thus more predictable. I'm much less likely to get lost, and so I'll reliably reach my destination in a far shorter time frame. Along the way, my goal may change. I may decide I want to go to San Francisco instead of San Diego. With a few adjustments, my map will get me there effectively and efficiently.

It's the same with a business. You can certainly start one up without a business plan, just as you can start a road trip without a map. You still may get lost with that plan in hand, but you can get right back on track, or make the necessary adjustments to course-correct. And if your goals change, you can reroute or pivot your business direction that much more easily. Just as with a map, the better your business plan is, the higher probability you have that you'll make what you need to give you the lifestyle you want now and in the future.

Yet, I have rarely seen a small business established in which there has been any substantive advance planning done, or that takes into consideration the founder's personal financial wants and needs, even though these people who start businesses are accomplished and intelligent. I have very good college friends who have been in business for nearly eighteen years. They're on their third enterprise; they'd started others previously that stumbled and fell, and had to close them. They have lost millions of dollars of income and opportunity, maybe even tens of millions of dollars, in these failures over the years, and now they're in the process of wrapping up their third string of businesses. And, if you were to ask to see their personal financial plan or business plan, they'd have none.

I work with a multi-million-dollar medical device company. They probably gross $10 million-plus per year, and they sold 51 percent of their business this past year. One great thing about the physician who started it is that he listens to his experts. I've worked with him for twenty years; he's consistently surrounded himself with the best people—a "Championship Team of Experts"—and has always been on top of his personal and business financial plans. When I sat in on the meeting between him and his buyers, they kept asking him for information, and invariably he had the numbers they wanted at his fingertips. They were blown away—one of them said, "It's very rare for us to meet with someone on the other side of a business that's this well-informed." Needless to say, he got the price he was looking for and achieved his financial plan.

If success means having you the life you want, your business must produce the wealth you need to accomplish your personal goals. It would also be great to like what you do, because if you're working in a field you don't like, you're not going to be happy. It's possible to put too much emphasis on passion, of course, and I often speak with business owners who confess to earning a lot but not liking their business. I also talk with owners longing for a simpler life, especially if they're having financial problems. But if you own a business, you get to say how you conduct it and how much it makes. And if it does not, you have the choice to leave it, pivot, or start another business.

Business and life are both inherently complex. They can be difficult and frustrating many days. But if they aren't going the way you want, you can change them. Like most important things we deal with as adults, you need to be willing to push out of your comfort zone to live the life you want and have a chance to enjoy it.

AIM FOR THE TRIFECTA.

When you love the business you're in, that's a win. If that business provides you with the cash flow you need to live your lifestyle now, that's another win. If, in addition to those two things, you earn enough to grow the wealth you'll need to retire when you wish, that's the third win—the trifecta of success. I should point out that I meet very few business owners who experience the trifecta and who actually stop working. They continue to work in their business or do something else. Genuine financial independence means that when you walk into work you don't have to be there; it's your choice, and you have the option to do something else if you wish. Imagine being free to choose whether or not you want to work. Doesn't that sound great? Can't you feel the stress and anxiety washing away with that thought? If your business plan allows you to achieve those three goals, you're doing it right. If it doesn't, you need a better plan.

I've achieved my trifecta, and I believe that anyone can, barring some catastrophic personal or health problem. It's possible that you may have to choose two out of three—if, for instance, the business you're in isn't something you enjoy doing. If you have two of those three, you could still be okay. But if you only have one of those three going for you, it's likely you're going to change businesses, or the business may be affected to the extent that it either underperforms, or worse, goes under—and sooner rather than later.

Someone I met recently who understands this very well is Brandon Vallorani, whose book, *The Wolves and the Mandolin*, extols the importance of celebrating life's simple pleasures in a harsh world.

Brandon is very conscious of how fortunate he is, but the fact is that he's made his own luck with his hard work and passion. He revolutionized online marketing, and became wealthy doing it. Now he's free to pursue life's pleasures, and concentrate on his signature line of fine wines and cigars. That's what hitting the trifecta looks like.

WHY DO BUSINESSES FAIL?

According to the Bureau of Labor Statistics, 80 percent of businesses with employees will survive their first year in business, and only 66 percent of businesses with employees will survive their second year in business.[7]

There are so many reasons a business can go under. I've read the "top ten" lists and I would guess you have, too. But in my observation, the primary reason businesses go broke is that they fail to track and plan their cash flow. You can have the best idea, service, or product out there; you may have learned how to do or make this through working for a successful business as an employee, so you're confident you can imitate that success yourself. But if you don't properly track and plan your cash flow, you may have a high probability of being among those businesses that don't survive. Remember the story I shared about having to let go of half of my staff at my firm back in the '80s? We were grossing $2 million, which in today's dollars is closer to $5 million, yet we didn't have a budget. We didn't track or plan our cash flow needs. I "planned" my cash flow by watching the cash balance in my checkbook—"checkbook flow management" I call it. As long as the cash balance in the bank was fine, I assumed all was well. It wasn't until we nearly failed to due to lack of cash

---

7   Bureau of Labor Statistics, "Table 7: Survival of Private Sector Establishments by Opening Year," accessed 2018, https://www.bls.gov/bdm/us_age_naics_00_table7.txt.

that I created our first budget. It was a revelation to me to see where our money was actually going, and that running the company via checkbook management was not enough.

Another reason businesses fail is the lack of cash reserves in the bank. Adam Witty, the CEO of Advantage Media Group|ForbesBooks, is known to have said, "You should build a moat of cash around your business. It protects like nothing else." I learned to watch this very carefully. Your business should have at least one month's worth of expenses in the bank, preferably three to six months' worth. I depended on banks to be there for me when I needed them. I learned that banks are a great source of funds when the business is doing well but they are not your friends when times are tough. This is not a criticism of banks—they are not there to take the risks you take in business. They are there to supply funds and services without risk.

Starting a business is a lot like building a house: would you simply choose an empty lot and start buying bricks and two by fours? No, you'd start with an architectural plan. It's the same thing with a business: you've got to have more than merely a "build it and they will come" attitude. You need to have a plan and to execute it properly.

Poor execution of your plan is as dangerous as having no plan at all. With a plan, you have a way to track your business against what you expected or needed, but if you fail to use it, it's like the tree falling in the forest with nobody to hear it. Hiring the wrong people or providing

Poor execution of your plan is as dangerous as having no plan at all.

poor service to clients can also keep you from properly executing your plan.

The daunting startup failure statistics I quoted earlier don't take into account those people who simply give up and throw in the towel, exiting their businesses because they see failure on the horizon. Some people don't understand the hard work that starting a business will entail, and simply lose the will to continue. When they realize that they're putting in twelve to fourteen hour days instead of the comfortable eight they're used to as employees, they throw up their hands and sell or close the operation. It's true that starting a business is tough, but if you're planning properly, and if your personal financial plan is aligned with your business plan, you can keep your goals in mind and work incrementally toward financial independence. With that plan, you're steering the ship of the business toward the destination you want to reach, rather than the ship drifting along wherever the current take it.

In the '90s, my business had fully recovered, and we were doing well. Our firm was smaller—there were six members on my team, and we had about forty clients across eight states. At this point I'd been working for many years, starting in my father's bakery back when I was in junior high school, and I felt I'd earned the privilege of easing back on the stick a little. I decided to start taking half of each year off. So, from then until about 2007, I'd be in the office two weeks and out of the office two weeks. Sometimes I'd be out a month and be back a month. I traveled the world, and bought an apartment in Paris. I shaped my working life, how my business operated, to suit the way in which I wished to live. I knew what I wanted, and what it would take for the business to afford me that lifestyle. I had a personal financial plan and I made the business plan follow it.

Remember that successful tax accountant I mentioned earlier who longed to be a social worker? Even though she was pulling down close to $700,000 per year, she wanted to close up shop because she hated the deadline-driven nature of the work, and because she hadn't set up the business to allow her to have time off during tax season. She wanted to be a social worker because she saw it as a more simple and rewarding life. Remember, I started a firm as a tax CPA—I had those deadlines too. But I said, "The heck with this. I'm not living my life this way." I started a tax division and I hired people to do those tasks for me, so that I could stick with my two weeks on/two weeks off schedule, even during tax season, without the quality of our work suffering.

It's a question of knowing what you want and achieving balance. I make sure that my business is running profitably, and that both our team and our clients are being taken care of. But I also make room for the things that make life worth living for me: being with family, traveling, reading, writing, cooking, and doing charitable work.

You don't have to resign yourself to an unhappy status quo; you just have to take the time to place into writing a plan that fits your personal goals as well as your business goals. I'm a big believer that you can make any business conform to what you want out of life, as long as you have the focus, mission and desire to do it. Sometimes there are sacrifices along the way, or you have to pivot when things don't go the way you want. But as long as you keep your eye on the target and focus your strategies on reaching your ultimate goal—living the lifestyle you

You can make any business conform to what you want out of life, as long as you have the focus, mission and desire to do it.

want now and in the future—there's a far higher probability you'll get there.

What can hinder you from achieving that goal? We'll talk about some of those obstacles in the next chapter.

Chapter 1 Takeaways

- The way you choose to run your business and the cash flow result are going to determine the way you live now and in the future.

- You want to be able to dictate the business's life, not the other way around. Everything begins with a sound financial plan. Failure to properly execute that plan is as bad as not having one.

- You can certainly start without a business plan, just as you can start a road trip without a map. But with a good map, or a solid plan, it's easier to course-correct, get back on track, and arrive where and when you want.

- The primary reason businesses go broke is that they fail to plan and track their cash flow.

- Focus your strategies on reaching your ultimate goal— living the lifestyle you want now and in the future—and there's a far higher probability you'll reach it.

CHAPTER TWO

THE OBSTACLES: WHY YOUR BUSINESS ISN'T PRODUCING THE CASH FLOW YOU NEED

"By prevailing over all obstacles and distractions, one may unfailingly arrive at this chosen goal or destination."
—Christopher Columbus

What stands between you and meeting your goals? What gets in the way of making the kinds of smart choices that empower your business to provide you with the lifestyle you want now and in the future?

I call these blocks obstacles—they're the thoughts or ideas that people have about money that prevent them from making better financial choices. What are these obstacles? There are actually two categories of obstacles: the practical obstacles, and the emotional obstacles.

THE PRACTICAL OBSTACLES

There are four kinds of practical obstacles: (1) no specific cash flow goal, (2) no written business plan, (3) no execution, and (4) no monitoring of your finances and reserves.

I. NO SPECIFIC CASH FLOW GOAL

So often, business owners just cross their fingers with a "Whatever happens, happens," point of view and expect that things will go as they hope, rather than doing the work of figuring out what they need the bottom line to be and then working their way backward toward that goal. This is a fatal mistake. You must know specifically what cash flow you need, and that number comes directly from your personal financial plan. If you need $500,000 of after-tax cash flow to live per year, then you know what the business has to produce. If the business is going to produce less than that after taxes, you're not going to live the lifestyle you want now or when you retire. Karyn Buxman, renowned keynote speaker, "neurohumorist," and author of many books including the upcoming *Funny Means Money*, hits the nail on the head: "No money, no mission. If you are out to achieve your dreams, maybe change the world, you won't get there without cash flow. And this is no joking matter!"[8]

2. NO WRITTEN BUSINESS PLAN

I certainly whiffed on this one in my initial outing as a business owner; I didn't have a plan in writing for the first five years I was in business, and in retrospect that was a big contributor to my subsequent difficulties. Having your financial plan written down—a plan that covers at least two to five years—provides that essential road

---

8   Karyn Buxman, interview with author.

map for how to get from where you are to where you wish to be. Without it, you're wandering. I was lucky to survive not having one. Will you?

3. NO EXECUTION

"Execution" means understanding exactly how you will produce and distribute the product or service you're intending to sell. How are you going to service your clients? How are you going to build your product? How are you going to deliver it? Your processes must be efficient, effective, and consistent, reliably giving your clients or customers the same great experience time and time again. Per-

Having your financial plan written down—a plan that covers at least two to five years—provides that essential roadmap for how to get from where you are to where you wish to be. Without it, you're wandering.

sonally, I've been following Michael Gerber's prescription for success in his book, *The E-Myth*, religiously for years. In our company, everything is process-oriented. From the first time a person comes into our office and every time thereafter, pad and pencils and trivets are always in the same places. There are no surprises. That creates a comfort level for our clients that they appreciate.

Do you have processes in place that dictate the quality of your customer's experience? If you don't, you need to create those processes, write them down, and make certain that everyone who interacts with customers is clear on them and following them to the letter. You'll find having these processes documented is also a terrific help when you're training or on-boarding new employees.

4. NO MONITORING OF YOUR FINANCES AND RESERVES

How do you measure success, or stave off potential failure? You do this by setting benchmarks, then properly monitoring your company's performance. Ask yourself periodically, "Where on the road map during the year am I, and what do I have to change to hit the goal(s) for the year? How do I have to pivot?

"Did I meet the goals I set in September? Whether it's selling a certain number of cars, or how many financial plans I've delivered, how close I am to meeting my benchmarks for success, what's the rest of the year going to look like? What do I have to change? If I don't have profitability, do I have to cut something? If I'm doing well in profits, should I invest in something else to make more profit? What are my expenses? Are they in line with what I predicted? If not, what must I adjust so that I can make meet my goals from a cash standpoint?"

These key performance indicators (KPIs) are your business's vital signs. If you're not keeping close and regular tabs on them, you won't be able to make the adjustments necessary to stay on track.

This monitoring process is what every well-run business in the world does, whether that's Facebook or Johnson & Johnson or the local small business. They're buying and selling divisions, adding people, firing people, and watching expenses—all so that they can stay in alignment with their ultimate profit goals. The problem I see for many smaller enterprises is that the people work so hard they don't make time to monitor; they simply hope the results they want will be there. The problem with counting on hope is that it gives you no leeway to make course adjustments during the year that could potentially save you from having to work longer and harder in life, or losing your business.

THE EMOTIONAL OBSTACLES

These are the thoughts we have concerning finance and cash flow that keep you from achieving your business plan. These thoughts prevent you from making the best decisions and achieving the wealth you need in life. Here are seven big emotional obstacles:

I. FEAR

Fear is a business killer. Fear is a dream killer. While practical obstacles can damage the prospects of a successful business and certainly affect the cash flow you need to live the lifestyle you want now and in the future, fear is the most damaging of emotional obstacles. What are some fears you might have?

Fear of Change

If you're obstinately resistant to change (i.e., "We have always done it this way"), that can hamper your company's growth and potentially lead to failure. Some people who are afraid of change hold the attitude that, "I have a business that's running well today. Let's leave well enough alone." That is fine, but keep in mind that, in the business world, things change all the time. Our markets change; our customers and clients change. If you don't keep up with those changes, your business could find itself left in the dust by its competitors.

Fear of Making the Wrong Decision

Okay, you made poor decisions in the past. Maybe a previous expert on your team has burned you. Who hasn't? Even so, as a business owner, you have to find the strength to make decisions. Fear of making the wrong decision can lead to what's called *paralysis by analysis,* where people simply can't make a decision when one needs to be made, so they just put their heads down and hope whatever storm is at the door will blow by.

Inevitably, making decisions involves taking a risk, a calculated risk, but a risk even so. If you find that you just can't commit to a decision when one must be made, you might not be cut out to run a business. Personally, I can't stand the pace of technology. But on the other hand, I know I have to run a business, and I have to run it profitability and efficiently, so I make sure that I have the right people around me and that we're up to date with whatever technology we need. Everyone has a comfort zone and a discomfort zone; as business owners, we have to be able to push past those personal limits. Don't let your resistance to change keep your enterprise in the slow lane.

2. TIME

People often fall back on: "I don't have the time to do it." From their point of view, it's true; they're so busy working *in* the business that they don't have time to work *on* the business. You've got to make time, because being proactive can save you trouble down the line. What kind of improvements can you make? Are you having problems with one or two suppliers or customers or clients? Have you lost clients because you weren't sufficiently responsive to their needs? Have you lost key employees? People will send you signals when they're unhappy. Not always loud signals, but loud enough to be heard if you're paying attention. A lot of people assume that time is a practical obstacle. There are only so many hours in the day, so how can you stretch it? You might find it strange to include time in the emotional obstacles, but think about how people always have the time to do what they want, or to act how they want, in an emergency.

A quick test: You are at work, and you're so busy that you don't have the time to take lunch. You don't have the time to speak with an important client. But, all of a sudden, you get a call from home that Sally has fallen off her bike, and your spouse had to take her to the hospital and needs you. Would you tell your spouse, "Sorry, I don't have time for that"? I doubt it. More likely your response will be, "Drop everything; I'm going to see Sally." It's a question of priorities, and if you don't make important things high priority, they don't get done. Working *on* the business is a high priority

3. LACK OF TRUST

How does lack of trust manifest itself? Sometimes there's a lack of trust around the advice that a business owner is getting from their outside advisors, because they've been burned before. Some just can't bring themselves to delegate; they're always certain they can do whatever it is better and faster. The fact is that nobody working for you is ever going to learn to do a thing as well as you do, if you don't give them that opportunity. Meaning: you'll be stuck doing every-thing yourself, instead of having the time to do the things only you as the business owner or leader can do to grow your business.

4. LACK OF KNOWLEDGE

People often know less than they think they do in business, and fail to seek out the knowledge they need. According to a July 2016 article in *Fortune*, two-thirds of Americans could not pass a basic financial literacy test.[9] It is no wonder: we graduate as some of the best engi-neering, legal, medical, and financial minds in the world, but we

---

9   Madeline Farber, "Nearly Two-Thirds of Americans Can't Pass a Basic Test of Financial Literacy," *Fortune*, July 12, 2016, http://fortune.com/2016/07/12/financial-literacy/.

do not teach basic finance in high school or college. Some business owners assume they understand this stuff well enough already. They are intelligent, aren't they? Unfortunately, intelligence doesn't necessarily correlate to financial literacy and comprehension, and these smart owners make mistakes when they fail to enlist their team of experts.

Another issue around lack of knowledge is "looking good." Nobody—especially not a business leader—wants to be wrong. It's human nature to want to look good. But sometimes we have to be big enough to admit we don't know everything, and asking for help is tough for many people, particularly those who are highly self-reliant and self-made.

If asking for help isn't your strong suit, here are two good reasons to start asking: First of all, you might learn a better way to do something. Second, it allows the people around you to contribute, and that makes them feel good about themselves and their work, which will only serve to boost your success.

5. GOING WITH YOUR GUT

Don't act on impulse or because your "gut" is telling you something's a good idea. Do your due diligence and research before you leap into any new venture, expansion, or acquisition. Look at the facts, engage your expert team to guide you, draw up a budget and a business plan. That will give you a much higher probability of success than blindly following your "gut."

6. RUSHING TO PAY OFF DEBT

Businesses commonly make a mistake that adversely affects their cash flow, which is paying debt off too quickly. I had a client whose business was doing very well, yet the four partners were suddenly feeling pinched. This was a business that generated top-line revenue of close to $10 million a year, but somehow the cash flow had slowed, and they weren't able to fund their pension plan.

When I looked at their cash flow, one of the first things I saw is that they had bought some equipment in the previous year that cost $2 million. They'd gone to the bank to get a three-year loan on it. Why? Because they came from the old school, "Let's pay this off as quickly as possible," way of thinking about debt. Mind you, this equipment had a life of ten years or more, but they wanted to pay it off very quickly. Now they were paying out about $700,000 a year—and they wondered why they were short on cash! I advised them to go back to the bank and take out a ten-year loan. They did that, and subsequently were only paying off $200,000 a year, plus interest. Voila! Suddenly their cash flow was back to near normal, and they were able to fund their pension plan.

Before you leap into quickly retiring business debt, run the numbers. How is it going to affect your goals? How's it going to affect your business plan? What's it going to do to your cash flow? Too many small businesses just don't run the numbers.

7. SAVING MONEY IN THE WRONG PLACES

Starting a business can mean eating a lot of ramen noodles at the beginning, but some business owners never lose their taste for frugality, and it winds up costing them, especially when it means hiring a cheap advisor or doing without financial advice altogether. Can you really afford bad advice, especially when it comes to your finances? Cut costs somewhere that won't wind up costing you more than you save.

Emotional obstacles are tough, because in many cases, they're effectively built in. Some people love the rough and tumble of business, but many people fear it, even though they're in business. For them, the butterflies most of us experience early in our careers just never go away, and fear can wind up dictating the limits of their success.

You may always have fears of making the wrong decision. You may always have time and/or trust issues, or any of the other issues I've talked about. You will always have some sort of emotional obstacle. The point is to recognize that they are there, and to learn to deal with them. When you made your first speech, you were scared, but you handled it. You can breach the emotional barriers if you're willing to acknowledge them and to consciously change the script of your internal monologue.

There's a terrific book by Dr. David Zelman, who founded the Transitions Institute in Dallas. In his book, *If I Can, You Can,* he dissects the interior conversations we have with ourselves when we're stressed or fearful. He makes the point that if you ask marathon runners what the biggest barrier to winning is, they'll tell you it's what you're hearing in your mind: Are you going to make it? Are you going to finish or not? If you tell yourself you can't finish, you won't.

But these undermining interior voices can be silenced once you're aware of them, and you can change the script to support your success, rather than torpedoing it.

SPECIAL ISSUES IN FAMILY ENTERPRISES

Many business owners have difficulty imagining their business running without them at the helm, and their resistance to establishing a succession plan can be especially damaging in family businesses where personal and professional relationships overlap. I was working with a large family-owned business run by a father and son; the son was highly competent, and more than ready to step into his dad's shoes, but his father just couldn't let go. He had a fear of losing control, and thus he couldn't bring himself to discuss with his son what the succession plan was and where he fit into it. It was affecting the performance of the business and pulling the family apart, because the son could see his father didn't trust him on some level. I had to sit them both down and help them to have a substantive and honest talk about their feelings. They also employed a great succession coach as part of their expert team. It was pointed out to the father that the business he loved so much could be in jeopardy if he failed to have a succession plan in place. What if he were unexpectedly incapacitated? The business would be left leaderless and rudderless, which would mean the loss of the family's greatest asset.

His coach and I were able to show him that his family, team, and clients deserved to know how and when the leadership of the family business would pass down. It took three or four years for him to relinquish the leadership role, but finally he did, and the business prospered under his son's guidance. Their relationship prospered also.

In other cases, the parent very much wants their child to step into their leadership role, but the adult child wants no part of the business, or simply lacks the talent for it. If you force your child into a role they don't want, that imperils not only the firm, but also puts the careers of executives and staff in jeopardy, and compromises the welfare of your clients and your family who are also involved. I've also seen situations in which the adult child lacked the skills and temperament necessary to lead, and had to be fired by their own parent.

It was the right decision for the business and the family as a whole, but they have not spoken since.

Sometimes long-term employees can become family, and as an employer you may keep them on payroll for much longer than you should. That can be expensive, and if the person isn't performing well, keeping them can also set a bad example for the rest of your team. When business is good, you may not feel the drag of under-performing employees. But when things get tight, it exposes all of those weaknesses, and you may be forced to make a tough decision under duress.

The emotional obstacles are tough to recognize, and require a high degree of honesty and self-reflection to overcome. What can help you handle your emotional obstacles? One important component is having a championship team of experts you can count on for advice—experts both within and outside of your company.

Chapter 2 Takeaways

- Obstacles stop us from being financially successful; they're the thoughts or ideas that people have about money that prevent them from making better financial choices.

- There are four *practical* obstacles:

    1. No specific cash flow goal (a "whatever happens, happens" point of view).

    2. No written business plan.

    3. No execution of the plan.

    4. No monitoring of your finances and reserves.

- The *emotional* obstacles are the thoughts we have concerning finance and cash flow that keep us from achieving our business plans. Amongst these are:

  - fear of change or of making the wrong decision;

  - failure to make time to work on the business, not just in the business;

  - lack of trust;

  - lack of knowledge;

  - going with your gut;

  - being too quick to pay off debt; and

  - saving money in the wrong places.

- Family businesses may also have to deal with emotional issues around control and succession that can complicate the business. Often an advisor and/or a coach can step in and help you to resolve the problem.

CHAPTER THREE

CREATE A CHAMPIONSHIP TEAM OF EXPERTS (INSIDE AND OUTSIDE YOUR BUSINESS)

"It's better to hang out with people better than you."
—Warren Buffet

Who do you listen to when it comes to advice on business decisions? Having less than competent advisors in key roles can cost you dearly.

Two clients of mine found this out in a pretty dramatic way. Chuck and Rob were highly successful and accomplished business owners who had started a series of companies over a ten-year stretch of time. They were relying on an accounting firm—actually a very sizable and reputable accounting firm—to plan and file the income tax returns for all of their companies and themselves. Unbeknownst to them, the accounting firm had actually gotten three years behind.

And to add insult to injury, they'd charged them for those three years, but the firm had not filed their taxes! It should be noted that Chuck and Rob should have realized this. At their request, we came aboard and performed a review of another seven years before the unfiled returns in question. We uncovered literally hundreds of thousands of dollars of tax credits those accountants hadn't taken. We had to eventually file over a hundred tax returns that had not been filed correctly to get some of that money back for them.

On another occasion, I attended a closing with a client for a piece of business real estate he was buying. I looked at closing statement and discovered $50,000 worth of mistakes my client would've been stuck paying for had he signed off on that particular statement. Clearly his real estate attorney had shunted the work off to a very junior employee, and it could have cost him dearly.

Another one of my clients who was applying for a loan worked with a banker who always promised to deliver work on time, but never delivered as promised. The same bank would request the same financial information over and over again, even though my client had already sent it. Beyond being irritating, it was a waste of time for this client. In the end, the bank changed the terms of the loan because they were so late and interest rates had changed. My client eventually fired them.

It's not only outside experts like accountants, attorneys, and bankers that can cost you money and time if they're less than professional; your in-house experts can be just as bad. I had a client whose office manager was stealing from him. We discovered it when he came to me saying, "I don't know why my cash flow is down." I told him that business had slowed down, collections were not being handled properly, or someone was stealing from him. We discovered that his office manager had opened up fake accounts and would steal checks as they came in. The same kind of thing occurred with another client whose comptroller had put a couple of phony employees on the payroll. We caught him before he was able to tap into the reserves of cash that were his real target. When my client had him arrested, we discovered he'd done the same thing at two previous jobs! Clearly, there was a failure to do due diligence on this guy when he was hired.

Daniel Chartock, entrepreneur and chief executive officer at Logical Attitude Enterprises, saw his enterprise go under because of an unscrupulous partner whom he'd trusted to run the business while he himself was still working in a corporate job at another company: "We were doing well—$3 to $5 million a year—but I had a business partner who took millions of dollars of loans out of the business in my name, using merchant cash advance companies, which ultimately pushed me into personal bankruptcy. He disappeared, and I had to start all over again."

No business can afford to have inept or outright unscrupulous players on its team of advisors. One way or another, they'll cost you money, and generally much more money than you'd have spent on hiring better people. What all of these business owners needed was a Championship Team of Experts. You do, too.

WHAT IS A CHAMPIONSHIP TEAM OF EXPERTS?

If you are a sports fan, you know that there always seems to be one team in the league that seems to do well each year. George Steinbrenner and the Yankees during his tenure is a prime example: they always were in contention, winning eight World Series Championships along the way. Other teams could not match that. Why? Steinbrenner always got the best players at all positions. If you didn't live up to playing at championship caliber, he found someone else. You should have a Championship Team for you and your business.

WHAT KINDS OF ROLES DOES YOUR CHAMPIONSHIP TEAM FILL?

For an individual, their team might include a CPA, attorney, banker, and an insurance agent among others. For a business, it might also include consultants, payroll services, pension experts, recruiters and more.

Internally the roles might include an office manager, and an accounts payable or accounts receivable person. If you're a larger company, it would probably include your C-suite people—the president, CEO, COO, and CFO. If you don't have championship-caliber people in these roles, they will end up costing you money, or perhaps even the business. One of my clients, the founder and CEO of his business, found out the caliber of his company president when he discovered that he was in the process of opening up a competing firm!

BE CAREFUL ABOUT WHO AND HOW YOU HIRE.

As businesses get bigger, they tend to take the individuals who excel in their roles and promote them up the chain—but the person who did such a great job as an accounts payable clerk might not have the expertise for the new and more important role you promote them into. Sometimes, businesses grow beyond the capabilities of these people, but their employer will keep moving them up until they're overwhelmed and failing in their roles. This can do great damage, not only to the career of that individual but also to your company.

Sometimes a couple will start a business together. Let's say the wife is the driver of the business, and the husband is just there to help out. The business grows and grows and maybe the husband becomes the office manager, but eventually the job's demands expand beyond his abilities. Understandably, his wife may be reticent to fire him, even though he's hurting the business. Whenever I'm called in to work with a husband and wife business, my first concern is how well they're working together and whether one of them is out of his or her depth in their job. Have they got to the point where one of them needs to leave? Many times, I've had to advise that one of the spouses must leave the company.

I had a client with an employee who'd started as a low-level clerk and worked his way up. He was a loyal team member, but when the firm got sizable, this guy wanted to be the chief financial officer of the company. My client was thinking seriously about giving him the job. I pulled him aside and said, "You've got to be kidding me; he doesn't have the talent or the skill set for that job." At this client's request, I explained this to the employee. While he didn't agree, he appreciated the fact that someone would at least be honest with him. And my client hired a great CFO.

If you're building a championship team within your organization, it's critical to thoroughly interview and vet your candidates: be slow to hire but fast to fire.

Poor team members literally cost you money. According to some estimates, up to three times their salary in a given year. A bad team is a ball and chain on a business. You can't progress with them. You can't rise to the level of client service you want to deliver. You lose cash flow because of their ineptitude, so that you can't expand the business as you might wish. The bottom line is that it will cost you years of life in terms of working more hours to make up for them.

You won't be able to get the value you want for the business in the time frame you're shooting for. You may not be able to become financially independent as quickly as you'd hoped.

Bad hires can also cost you your company's good reputation. You want people to be saying, "They take good care of me and really bring us a great product," not "They never return phone calls, they're late with their work, and they make too many mistakes." That kind of review can kill your company.

Keep in mind that when you're not getting the cash flow the business should produce, the problem is not just that you can't save more or you may not be able to afford the lifestyle you wish to have now or in the future, poor cash flow also hurts the value of the business. If you're not producing what you should be because of team incompetence, you'll get less for your business when you sell it, which can hurt your personal financial plan.

HOW CAN YOU FIND A CHAMPIONSHIP CALIBER TEAM MEMBER?

Begin with a great process for finding, interviewing, and vetting potential team members. I strongly recommend the book *Who: A Method for Hiring* by Geoff Smart and Randy Street. Using their straightforward, commonsense methods can lower the odds that you'll hire the wrong person. You should also consider hiring a top-flight recruiter, particularly if you're trying to fill executive level positions. Having a partnership with a professional on that level can allow you to grow a great championship team.

Generally speaking, it's a good idea to avoid hiring friends and relatives, because it makes it harder to fire the person if they're not up to the job you've put them in. I don't know how many times I've seen businesses struggle with having to fire a son or daughter, because it creates a family rift. It can work—there are many successful family enterprises, but clarity on expectations on both sides is crucial from the beginning.

"Know when you have someone who's playing football when you're playing basketball"—I learned that thirty years ago from Sharon Tiger, a team building consultant who came into my business and told me, "There are a lot of good people out there, but just because they're talented and have the skill sets and the personality you want, don't assume they've bought into your business or your mission. They may privately think, 'I could do things better.'" Working with an employee like that, particularly in a key role, is like managing a basketball team that has a football player on its roster. They're just not going to have their heads in the game, and it can only hurt the team.

DON'T NEGLECT ANNUAL EVALUATIONS.

Whether it's your internal team or your external team, it's necessary to the smooth running of your business to evaluate them on at least an annual basis—you need to know when to hold 'em, and know when to fold 'em. I suggest taking the test on the next page annually, so you have a clear idea of where your team is strong or weak. How does your team stack up? Take this simple but revealing test.

On a piece of paper, list your internal team by name and position. Next to their name, give them a rating of A, B, or C.

A is for the superstar: They always finish their work on time, they answer phone calls promptly, they've showed you ways to save money with them, or they just give sound advice. They care. They are enthusiastic. These are the keepers on your team.

B is for the person who is okay—not great, but adequate. They are spotty on returning phone calls, or maybe they miss deadlines once in a while. While they might be a nice person, you would replace them if someone better came along.

C is for the team member who's always a day late and a dollar short. They never return calls in a timely way, never get back to you with an answer to a question, and are always late with work. You always have to follow up with them. You can't trust them with assignments. These team members cost you money, and sometimes a lot of money. They are a drag on your efforts to get ahead financially. These C-grade members need to be fired.

Assessing your internal team every year with this test is an easy way to potentially find more wealth. It is hard enough to find cash flow to live the life you want now as well as to save for retirement. Even if you're already financially independent, you don't need to waste your hard-earned wealth carrying poor team members. Of course, if the C-grade person is a good friend or relative, you might choose to keep them on the payroll. Just know that they might be retired while you're still working to make up for having taken their poor advice!

This should also be a mandatory exercise with your team of experts outside the company, or for your personal team—your insurance agent, attorney, banker, and CPA. Do they do their work on time, and promptly return phone calls? Do they give you valuable information? They're keepers. Bs are the ones that are just okay, but when better experts come along, replace them. Cs, you fire.

I was on the phone with a person recently who read my previous book. She has her own business, and had called me with some questions. She told me about the CPA who she'd been using for two years; the first year he'd done a great job on her returns, filing them promptly and finding her some substantial tax savings. But the second year, he called her on April 12 to say, "I'm going to have to extend your return." She was surprised, and asked how much she was going to owe. He said, "I can't tell you that. I'm just going to put you on an extension and you can pay it later." When he finally filed another two or three months later, she owed $50,000, which means she also had to pay substantial penalties to the IRS and the state. When she pointed that out to him, he didn't even apologize, he just made excuses. She asked, "Al, what do you think I should do with the guy?"

I said, "He's a C-player on your team; fire him." She did.

When you're just starting out in business, you generally rely on your personal network to help you pull your team of outside experts together. You'll ask friends or family for recommendations, or you'll use a friend, or your old college roommate. But you have to know when you've outgrown them. You may have started off with a Mom-and-Pop operation, but now you have a hundred employees. That accountant you've had with you since you started may not be up to the sophistication of the operation you have today. It's tough to tell a friend, "Look, thank you for your services, but I'm using someone else." Just remember that your only option is to accept the losses they'll inevitably cost you, and plan on working longer.

Of course, it's not necessary to have the best team of people around you at work—or even a championship team of experts outside your business—if you *want* to work longer and harder and are willing to risk not having the lifestyle you want. When you think about it in those terms, what seems like the smarter choice?

Personally, I learned this lesson a long time ago. When I first started my business, I didn't value advice as much. I just wanted to get things done and I wanted to save money. Typically, I picked the cheapest person, because I assumed, "They're all about the same." It wasn't until I saw the errors being made that I began to understand what the lack of good advice was costing me, and that changed the way I looked at hiring and firing. It was an expensive but extremely valuable lesson.

Chapter 3 Takeaways

- Having less-than-competent advisors in key roles can sentence you to working longer and having less.

- For an individual, your team might include a CPA, attorney, banker, and insurance agent among others; for a business, it might also include consultants, payroll services, pension experts, and recruiters and more.

- As businesses grow they tend to promote people to a level of incompetence. The person who did such a great job as an accounts payable clerk might not have the expertise for this new and more important role.

- If you're building a championship team within your organization, be slow to hire, but fast to fire.

- Begin with a great process for finding, interviewing, and vetting potential team members.

- Generally speaking, it's a good idea to avoid hiring friends and relations.

- Fire C-players immediately. They're costing you money.

CHAPTER FOUR

BECOMING THE MASTER OF THE CASH FLOW OF YOUR BUSINESS

*"Start by doing what's necessary; Then do what's
possible and suddenly you are doing the impossible."*
—St. Francis of Assisi

I n a conversation with Damon Gersh, founder of many businesses and philanthropic organizations, I smiled when he said, "Happiness is a positive cash flow." While he gave due credit to venture capitalist Fred Adler for the quote, he added, "Make sure your business model is one that supports cash flow generation so you can seize opportunities, grow your business, make money, and have peace of mind."

Why do so many businesses get into trouble with cash flow? Sometimes it's the lack of basic financial literacy, but in my observations, it's very often because the business owner doesn't understand the concept of cash flow funnels. Whether you're a startup, or your established business is undergoing a period of rapid growth, if you make better financial decisions and learn to master your cash flow, then you'll waste less money on avoidable expenses and will give less money to the government. That will empower you to use that money to grow your business, to have the lifestyle you want to have now, to save and/or build your wealth for how you want to live in retirement, and to achieve financial independence. When we talk about finding more cash flow for individuals, we call it the Integrated Cash Flow Management Approach™. When we're talking about businesses, we call finding more cash flow Multiple Wealth Drivers.

THE FUNNELS

The analogy I use to describe how most people think about business cash flow is the "Three Funnel System," or simply, "The Funnels."

Most people think of the cash flowing into their businesses as though it's coming to them through a series of funnels. The first funnel this money passes through for a business represents what happens when income taxes are taken out of a business's income.

The second funnel the business's income passes through is debt: amounts owed to a bank for business loans or equipment, or on personal credit cards, or personal loans.

This remaining money then flows through the third funnel, which represents operating expenses for the business—rent, cost of labor, and materials.

CASH FLOW FUNNELS

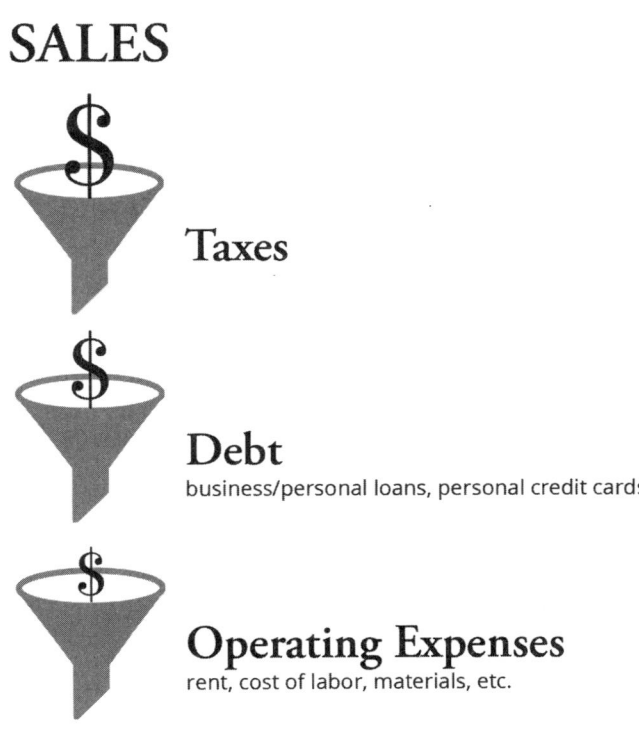

SALES

Taxes

Debt
business/personal loans, personal credit cards

Operating Expenses
rent, cost of labor, materials, etc.

$ **Free Cash Flow**
what you pay yourself/others—is it enough?

What's left after passing through the funnels is the money with which you pay yourself and other owners. This figure determines how you will build your wealth, and whether or not you'll be able to live the lifestyle you want, now and in the future.

In a well-run business, money is apportioned appropriately to cover taxes, debt service, and operating expenses. But I've seen a lot of businesses get into trouble because they effectively "rob Peter to pay Paul" by not putting sufficient money aside throughout the year to cover their taxes, especially if it's their first really good year. They'll go to their accountant for tax preparation at the end of it and are astonished when he tells them, "You owe $75,000," and they don't have the cash put aside to cover it because they didn't plan their cash flow properly.

Owners of a well-run business will make sure that what's left will be adequate to cover their salary, because they're clear on how much it takes to live the lifestyle they want. They'll also know how much they need to put aside from this money so they don't have to work longer than they want to, and will be able to afford to retire when they wish.

COMMON MISTAKES BUSINESSES MAKE: USING THE CHECKBOOK TO MANAGE CASH FLOW

How do businesses, both startups and established enterprises, wind up making costly mistakes in managing their cash flow?

The thing I see most often is they look to their checkbook as their only cash flow management tool. At the end of the month, they're looking at their balance, and asking, "Do I have enough money to make my payroll? Do I have enough to cover other bills?" There's really no formal process in place to look at how much they've spent during the month, or what they're likely to need to cover payroll and expenses for future months.

Ever heard the joke, "They were so successful, they went out of business?" It sounds counterintuitive, but it's true: you can have a business that's chugging along, doing fairly well, and then suddenly it may experience a surge in sales. That sounds like good news, but the way in which you manage your business cash flow—including billing customers in a timely fashion, collecting the money you're owed promptly, and making sure you have enough debt to cover some capital expenditures in the business—can make the difference between enjoying continued success or locking your doors for good. The orders may be pouring in, and you can be making a profit on paper, but your cash flow crunch can still be so egregious that you can't pay your employees or your vendors.

I don't care whether it's a $1 million business, a $10 million business, or even a $100 million business; if cash flow is not managed properly, you're risking the health of your enterprise. I'm not just talking about your current cash flow, or what's in your checking account, but what level of cash flow will be there in one month, two months, or five months down the road. If you're not diligently monitoring cash flow, or having someone assist you in planning for these eventualities, you face the risk of having a very successful business that goes broke because you can't afford to keep it.

I don't care whether it's a $1 million business, a $10 million business, or even a $100 million business; if cash flow is not managed properly, you're risking the health of your enterprise.

Entrepreneur Rick Sapio sees this another way: "Most gurus teach revenue growth, or profit growth, but virtually no one is teaching cash-flow growth and management. We were investors in a business that had record revenue growth of 80 percent per year for three years in a row. Little did we know that the business was facing bankruptcy, because although revenue was growing exponentially, they were selling money-losing products."[10]

---

10   Interview with Rick Sapio, op. cit.

TAKING THE REINS

What does it require to plan intelligently and effectively for your business cash flow? I'm not suggesting you need to get a degree in accounting or that you need to invest in expensive accounting software. A good place to start with a small business is simply taking out a sheet of paper and saying, "For this month, I project that this much income will come in; these are my expenses, and this is what I've put aside for taxes, for myself," etc. That's how you begin making a projection. Then, at the end of the month, you go back and see how well you did. Were your predictions accurate? Did the amount of money you anticipated actually come in? Did those expenses occur as you'd planned? Were you able to pay all your bills? Did you have excess cash flow?

As rudimentary as this process is, it's a good first step. Many people just do this kind of planning using an Excel spreadsheet program. They look at the cash they start with, then they list all the expenses they anticipate for that month and the income they think is going to come in. Again, it's not extremely detailed, but in aggregate it allows them to see whether they're likely to be able to pay their business expenses and bills, and whether their cash flow will be adequate to cover them.

Start with this exercise for the current month, and try to project numbers for the next three months, whether on paper or on an Excel spreadsheet. One month could be positive, the next negative, but over a series of months, you will see if you have the cash flow over time to offset poor months. This begins to give you an inkling as to whether you're likely to come up against a cash flow problem in the near future, and that gives you time to do something about it. You might have to take action to decrease expenses, or recognize that you have to bring in more income.

I do this religiously for my own company: I sit down with my internal financial team and together we forecast our cash flow for the twelve months of the year. However, you can begin with projecting cash flow for at least three months out. Here's a simple cash planning format to begin with:

WELL-RUN COMPANY
CASH FLOW PROJECTION
THREE MONTHS ENDING MONTH 31, 20XX

	Month 1	Month 2	Month 3
Sales Collected	$93,000	85,000	96,000
Monthly Business Expenses			
Rent	10,500	10,500	10,500
Payroll	35,000	35,000	35,000
Insurance	1,200	1,300	1,216
Payroll tax	3,600	3,600	3,600
Material for Production	5,000	5,000	5,000
Telephone	342	2,177	2,297
Software	3,428	2,176	2,296
Marketing	1,466	1,366	616
Postage/UPS	264	936	331
Legal	-	300	2,300
Loan Payment	2,300	2,300	2,300
Travel & Entertainment	1,214	1,943	671
Utilities	542	542	542
Total Projected Expenses	64,856	67,140	66,669
Net Cash Flow (Sales Less Total Expenses)	28,144	17,860	29,331
Cash for Owner (For Lifestyle, Taxes, Pension)	25,000	25,000	25,000
Net Cash Flow After All Expenses	$3,144	(7,140)	4,331

Possible actions for month 2: have employees work less hours, maybe order less material for production, look at what customers owe and see if collecting timely.

Take a sheet of paper and draw three columns: month one, month two, and month three. Predict the cash from sales you anticipate based on your experience or the orders you have in-house. Predicting income is the more difficult part. Predicting your expenses is easier. Take the total expenses from the total income and you will have net cash flow. But don't forget you! Subtract from the cash flow (or make it part of your expenses) what you need to live the lifestyle you wish, and what must be put aside for income taxes, and for pension or retirement. The net after this is the cash flow you are projecting.

Note that month two is negative. This will necessitate action on your part. Maybe you have to cut back your employees' hours. Maybe you don't need as much material. Or possibly the sales receipts have suffered because you did not stay on top of collections from customers. Now you have the beginnings of a system to avoid surprises and manage cash flow better. As time goes on, you can decide how sophisticated you wish to get with your cash projecting.

This projection process (with most eventually getting more complicated) is one we've put into place with almost every business client we have guided, large or small. One company I worked with manufactured industrial ceramic parts. They had been in business for a while and they were having cash flow issues. Why? A big part of the problem was that they didn't have a system to forecast where cash flow could be from month to month. If you don't know where you are, you don't know how to get where you're going, so we set up a cash flow management system for them tailored to their business that allowed them to make accurate projections around their costs and profits. Our firm and other well-run firms actually forecast this on a month-by-month basis for the entire year, but for a business that's not addressed this before, that might be too great a stretch at first, so their predictions and projections may be off the mark. It's like playing tennis: if you only play tennis once a year, you probably won't play well, and you'll feel awkward on the court. If you play once a month, you're going to play better than the person who only picks up a racquet once a year. If you start playing once or more a week, you may not ever be a champion, but you'll probably play pretty well.

Looking at cash flow as I've described here might feel odd at first, or hard to do, but you'll be surprised at how accurate your ability to forecast your cash flow will become over time, once you get into the habit of tracking on a regular basis, month to month, year to year. In the same way you become a master in your tennis game, you'll become a master of predicting the cash flow of your business.

Dean Minuto is an award-winning speaker and entrepreneur who most recently won the Sales Coach and Mentor Vistage Speaker of the Year Award, and who helps thousands of people get to "Yes" faster with his innovative program, YESCALATE. He's very clear about the importance of cash flow in his own business: "I've always said, 'if God blessed me with a son, I'd name him Cash. And his middle name would be Flow. There is nothing more important to keep in mind. Nothing else matters; not the quality of your product, nor how capable a marketer you are. Nothing tops cash flow." When asked what the most important advice was he'd ever had on cash flow, he said, "It came in two sets of words: 'plus expenses.' And 'payment up-front.' Those four words, two separate concepts, literally changed *everything.*"[11]

---

11   Dean Minuto, interview with author.

THE BREAKEVEN STATEMENT

There's a critical difference between cash flow and what shows up on your business's profit and loss statement, and this can get complicated. While your profit and loss statement could record your sales, that money doesn't necessarily show up as cash flow, because you may not have actually collected the money owed you by your customer. You may have accounts receivable or money owed to you. It depends how you account for income and expenses: cash versus accrual. To keep this simple, we will only deal with cash that is collected or paid out. However, knowing how production and sales collection operate in a business can have a major impact on your cash flow and, if not properly managed, leave you in a lurch.

Take as an example a fashion website that opens with a big sales campaign. To their jubilation, a thousand orders pour in. Now they've got to ship those orders to customers who are invoiced with delivery. They've got a thousand orders worth $100,000, but they haven't collected a dime. Meanwhile, they still have to pay for the expenses associated with producing the products. They have to pay employee salaries, employee benefits, taxes, marketing, and all the other costs of doing business. While they can have a profit and loss statement that states, "Sales of $100,000 and expenses of $75,000, leaving a $25,000 profit," that doesn't reflect their actual cash flow. That's why online retailers make sure they're paid at the time of sale—they want that cash flow to come to them more quickly.

As a company either grows or wants to manage their cash flow in a more sophisticated way, the sophistication of their accounting system has to change to match that. When a firm is trying to get control of their cash flow, but lacks a good process to do this, they can use a "breakeven statement." This is a simple way for a company to see where they stand with cash flow but also a little more sophisticated than that in my earlier illustration. This statement will allow you to delve deeper into issues around your cash flow. It can also allow you to compare your company to your peers' (if that information is available). This can reveal if you are running your company as well as or better than your competition, and if not, why not.

What is breaking even? To most people when they have a business, breaking even means covering their expenses. Monthly expenses are relatively easy to predict—like rent, utilities, and payroll—the more difficult thing to predict for most businesses is how much in sales or income they're going to get in that month. Most people would see this as, "I have $100,000 worth of expenses; I need at least $100,000 of income coming in from sales to break even," where they're covering just the cost of operating the business. But to me as a wealth advisor, that is not breaking even. To break even for that month, you also have to put two or three other things in the equation: you have to look beyond your expenses to the income you need to live the lifestyle you want. You also have to put money aside to pay your income taxes, and you have to contribute to your savings for your eventual retirement from the business, so that you can be financially independent someday.

So, let's assume that your monthly business expenses are $100,000. Let's say you need $25,000 to pay your personal bills for that month. You'll need to put aside another $10,000 for taxes. Then you have to also save in your pension plan and general savings account for retirement; let's say that's another $15,000. Now, you can see that your monthly breakeven is going to be closer to $150,000, which means you need a cash flow after expenses of $150,000.

The lesson is that when you're writing down your expenses to predict your cash flow, whether that's on a legal pad or in your Excel spreadsheet, you have to add in your personal expenses, taxes, and the amount you need to put aside for retirement or financial independence. If you're not doing that, you're not going to have an accurate accounting for what constitutes your breakeven point or what your business has to produce.

Data about your competitors is useful in measuring your own success or where you fall short. Every industry has metrics or key performance indicators—KPIs—that let them know how they stack up in terms of profitability as compared to their peers. No matter what business you're in, whether you own a large gourmet food store, a group of jewelry stores, or a chain of pharmacies, it's good to have these KPIs at hand when you're assessing the cash flow from your business, because they help you see where you're falling short.

UNDERSTANDING EXPENSES

When you're looking at cash flow going out or paying expenses, these costs can be classified as either *direct expenses* or *variable expenses*, also known as *indirect* or *fixed expenses*.

Direct expenses are expenses that are a direct result of your sales activity. For example, if you sold fifty thousand units this month, you had to pay X number of employees for X hours to support those sales or use materials in the production of your product, so X equals your direct/variable expenses. If your sales double the next month, your staff and materials costs are also going to rise in proportion to the sales, which is why they're called *variable* expenses. They vary with sales going up or down.

Fixed expenses aren't contingent on sales; if you have a loan, for instance, you're still going to pay the same amount of interest on it no matter what your sales were. Phone, electric and most other expenses not tied directly to sales do not generally vary much whether sales go up or down for the month.

Understanding the difference between direct/variable expenses and indirect/fixed expenses is very important, because if you see that in the future it's likely that your sales are going to be up or down, you may have to find ways to adjust your direct/fixed expenses to make sure you're going to reach the cash flow profits that you need to have. This is called a breakeven statement, because if your sales are only going to cover the variable and the fixed expenses with nothing left for owner expenses—your salary, health insurance, pension plan, etc.—you're not really breaking even.

USING YOUR BREAKEVEN STATEMENTS TO REACH THE FUTURE YOU WANT

In the illustration shown here, you see an example of a breakeven statement for a given month and year to date through June.

A well-run business looks at this monthly and on a cumulative basis. A good practice is to start looking at the far-right column where it says "year to date" and look at what the business did up to that time. You have just finished June and you would like to know what your business will do for the rest of the year, or what you want it to achieve. While a cash flow statement is important to avoid cash crunches, the breakeven statement allows you to see trends as months go by and to target the bottom line. Further, you can see what you did in the previous year from June on, and if you can improve in the second half of the year versus the same time period from the year prior.

WELL-RUN COMPANY

BREAKEVEN STATEMENT
FOR JUNE 20XX AND THE SIX MONTHS ENDING JUNE 30, 20XX

	For the Month		Year to Date	
	June 20XX	%	June 30, 20XX	%
Income (sales collected)	$100,000	100%	600,000	100%
Direct Expenses:				
Payroll	40,000	40%	210,000	35%
Material for production	7,500	8%	35,000	6%
Employee benefits	1,200	1%	7,800	1%
Payroll tax	3,600	4%	24,000	4%
Total direct expenses	52,300	**52%**	276,800	**46%**
Income after direct expenses	47,700	**48%**	323,200	**54%**
Indirect Expenses:				
Rent	10,500	11%	66,000	11%
Telephone	400	0%	2,800	0%
Software	3,500	4%	36,000	6%
Marketing	1,500	3%	10,500	3%
Postage/UPS	120	0%	720	0%
Legal	-	0%	2,300	0%
Loan payment	2,300	2%	13,800	2%
Travel and entertainment	1,200	1%	8,400	1%
Utilities	500	1%	3,000	1%
Total indirect expenses	20,020	20%	143,520	24%
Net income (after indirect expenses)	27,680	28%	179,680	30%
Net income before owner's compensation	25,000	25%	150,000	25%
Net breakeven income after all expenses	$2,680	3%	29,680	5%

When you get to November or December, you can start to use this to predict the next year or to budget. Your business will probably take in about $1.2 million by the end of the year. You want to improve upon that the next year but also look at how this will affect expenses and your bottom line.

When predicting your variable expenses for the next year you might see they are going up higher in percent than the income. This form gives you a process for seeing how much your income must go up to meet this expenses as well as maybe how to control them.

Then when looking at the next year, you move to your fixed expenses, and compare them to the previous year. Like the variable expenses, you can see how these might eventually affect the income the company must make to cover any increases in expenses and maybe make more profit.

Look at the trend in the illustration. Note that the June direct expense percent was higher then the percentage was over six months. Are labor costs getting out of control? Note the indirect expenses for the six months are higher percentage-wise than June. While a good sign, was this a fluke? Analyzing this information will allow you to take more effective action and to understand what is going on in your business.

Are your expenses likely to go up faster than your sales? If so, having this insight gives you the opportunity to make adjustments, whether in your spending, your sales, or both, to be sure that you'll garner the profit you want rather than having to settle for the profit you get.

Unfortunately, most businesses don't take the time to project what they want and need their profit to be in the coming year, but it is extremely important to have a target. Say you get up one day, look in the mirror and decide, "I've gained too much weight; I have to get on a health program." What's the best way to tackle it? First you need some metrics, to help you measure how to improve. Maybe you swim five laps a day, but by year's end you'd like to be able to do ten without stopping. You know you're twenty pounds overweight, and you'd like to lose that during the year. Now you've got a target and you can measure your progress.

On the other hand, if you just say, "I'll take better care of myself," you have no specific goal in mind, and no way to measure your progress, and you're less likely to follow through with your good intentions.

Your breakeven statement is like your financial health metrics. You can see all along the way every month whether you are on target. You can start breaking it down not only for the year, but on a per month basis, so that as you go through the year you can look at each month and say, "Did I hit my targets? If I didn't, why didn't I? What do I have to do?"

If you plan your cash flow using this format or another like it, while the first year may be a bit of a challenge, ultimately you will be able to predict your cash flow and profits so accurately you'll be amazed. I know this from my own experience, having been the owner of a multimillion-dollar business that for its first five years had no budget. It wasn't until the cash in the checking account wasn't there to cover payroll that I said, "I've got to get control over this." I remember when management got together and we sat down to make up that first budget. We were so off over the next year's projections it wasn't even funny. But I will tell you that after a couple of years, we were within single-digit percentage points in terms of accuracy.

Why does this matter? Because it puts you in the driver's seat, and you can force a better outcome by taking actions throughout the year that will allow you to meet your targets. That's how successful corporations like Apple operate; they look at their numbers every month throughout the year, and adjust accordingly. Don't think you have to be Apple to do this! The process is the same—they just have more zeroes behind their numbers. If you're looking at your cash flow statement and your breakeven, or profit loss statement at least every month, you'll quickly learn to make better predictions and give yourself the advantage of being able to make adjustments to get your company back on course. Having this analysis also allows well-run corporations to compare themselves to competitors to see if they are doing better than their peers or not as well, and why.

As you go into the next year, make sure that you or your accounting department is producing a financial statement, a cash flow statement, and a breakeven statement minimally once a month, within no more than four or five days after the end of the month. If you get to the first quarter and you're still way off, ask yourself, "Was I too optimistic in sales? Am I spending too much money here?" and calibrate accordingly.

In my case, as our firm grew, we established a board of advisors. We asked other CEOs of other companies to sit on our board and look at our operations and finances at least once per quarter. We gave them permission to tear us apart. Their input forced us to look very seriously at getting clarity around our targets and to focus on making the adjustments required to hit them.

If you're the owner of a business with employees, customers, and clients that depend on you, it's your responsibility to make sure the business is running properly. Even if you don't care about the money you're making for yourself, you want the business to be around for them. A profitable business is one that's going to be around for your team and for your clients.

THE CFO MIND-SET

If you want to become the master of your business's cash flow, you need to adopt what I call the CFO (chief financial officer) mind-set. Your business might be large enough to have a chief financial officer, or you may take on that role as the president and CEO. But whoever assumes this role must be looking at the business as a CFO does—with clear targets in mind, knowing what the return on equity needs to be, and understanding the key performance indicators or the metrics for the business or industry you're in. These goals must be defined in absolute numbers and percentages, not, "I think it's going to be about 10 percent this year," but rather "We're going to increase business 10.258 percent this year."

The CFO mind-set means identifying multiple success drivers. What is a success driver? A success driver looks for opportunities to reach the goals whenever they can find them. What opportunities are there to increase the revenues? What opportunities are there for cutting costs, using debt more effectively, or investing some of the capital for the future? Most business owners don't look at how things can be run more efficiently: they're too busy working *in* the business to work *on* the business. But the only job the CFO has every day is to serve that one client: the business. The business itself may have tens of thousands of clients, but they're being taken care of by the other people within the organization.

Having a CFO allows the organization to make well-informed financial choices. CFOs will think through the full impact of the choice they make. For example, say I want to open up another location, another factory, or another retail store. Most owners and entrepreneurs will see an opportunity and jump for it like squirrels chasing nuts, without fully considering the financial impact of that new investment. That's the CFO's job—to consider what that new location will make versus what it will cost, and whether it's going to be profitable.

Most people make decisions in a vacuum. I was dealing with a sizable company in New Jersey some years back whose owner was considering building a new production facility in the South. The CEO told me, "I think it's a great opportunity," but he had no real numbers to back that feeling up. He hadn't even begun to do the necessary deep dive into due diligence. For instance, could the facility actually be built in the location he'd chosen? What local laws might make that difficult? What was the available workforce? We convinced him that he needed to take on a CFO to help make decisions like this. He did so, and that person confirmed that the location he'd been looking at was a very poor choice. But business owners will sometimes just go ahead and make these kinds of decisions without the proper people around them to advise them. Too many bad decisions will shutter their businesses. Holding that CFO mind-set requires making well-informed decisions versus "going with your gut."

If your business is not large enough to have a CFO, you've either got to adopt that mind-set yourself or work with an expert in your company—for instance, an inside accountant or a bookkeeper—who can help you to set clear targets, find cash opportunities, make more informed decisions, and properly track your results.

Chapter 4 Takeaways

- Businesses run into cash flow problems because the business owner doesn't understand the concept of cash flow funnels.

- Once your money has passed through the funnels, what's left is the money with which you pay yourself and other owners to cover your lifestyle, income taxes, and for-retirement savings.

- Owners of a well-run business are clear on how much it takes to live the lifestyle they want now and in the future.

- Businesses run into trouble when they use their checkbooks as their primary cash flow management tool.

- You must have a breakeven statement, which is like your financial health metrics. This allows you to see every month whether you are on target to meet your goals.

- Have the CFO mind-set.

CHAPTER FIVE

THE WEALTH BUILDING FORMULA® FOR YOUR BUSINESS: A WAY TO MAKE THE 100 PERCENT CORRECT FINANCIAL DECISION, EVERY TIME

"If we did all of the things we are capable of,
we would literally astound ourselves."
—Thomas A. Edison

I n the previous chapter, I explained the CFO mind-set, also called our Integrated Cash Flow Management Approach™, and how to look at your financial choices as a well-run business should. But how can you, as an individual as well as a business owner, be sure that the choices you're making in your personal and business finances will support your ultimate goals, provide you with the lifestyle you want now, and create the wealth you need to retire from or sell your business when you want to?

Our methodology for doing this is the Wealth Building Formula®. Whether we're talking about your personal financial goals or your goals for your business, the Wealth Building Formula® gives you the knowledge you need to make the right decisions 100 percent of the time, every step of the way, and helps you make the decisions that will provide you with the lifestyle you want now, and the wealth you need to enjoy it in the future. There is a personal Wealth Building Formula® (I covered this in depth in my book *Master Your Cash Flow: The Key to Grow and Retain Wealth*) and a business Wealth Building Formula®, and you need to understand them both.

DO YOU KNOW YOUR BENCHMARKS?

Let's talk about benchmarks first. Benchmarks are what well-run companies have that badly-run ones don't. Apple and other successful companies, big or small, have financial benchmarks or KPIs that allow them to assess things like, "Are we doing better than our peers or worse than our peers? Are we hitting our targets?" Among their benchmarks might be earnings per share, return on equity, or other measures. Too often, business owners don't think in terms of targeted earnings, and most don't even know how much they need for themselves, the income taxes they must pay, or how much to save for retirement. They don't have a long-term investment return objective or know the rate of return needed from their investment portfolios to make it all work. They simply hope it's there, and that it will all work out somehow. For example, with investments, they look to see, "Did I do better than the S&P 500 this quarter?" That's not the same thing as creating your target. But you can't have a target without a plan that provides you with benchmarks and a way to make the right financial decisions consistently.

The Wealth Building Formula® allows people to put their goals into exact numbers. It creates a clear process by which they can make the best financial decisions—one that allows them to see where they are on their road map. How many years are they from financial independence? Are they on the right track? What adjustments could they make to get to that goal faster?

The Wealth Building Formula® looks at what cash flow you need today to live the life you wish sometime in the future. For example, let's assume you needed $750,000 a year to live—to pay your taxes, to cover expenses, and to save toward building your wealth. Someday, you want to have the option to leave that business, either to do something else or to retire. If you can get that same $750,000 you require every year from your investments, adjusted for inflation (you can count on inflation rising each year), then you're financially independent. You can do whatever you want.

The Wealth Building Formula® is Straightforward:

$C \times T \times \%$ Return = $$$

C is investable cash or the amount of wealth you need to generate cash flow.

T is the time frame in which you want to gain your financial independence for the rest of your life.

% Return is the long-term investment return objective that you need (from your investment portfolio or by finding more investable cash).

$$$ is the cash flow you need in today's dollars to live the life you want in the future.

You have to solve each component to make sure this all works and that the cash flow you are generating equals the cash flow that you'll need in today's dollars at the point when you retire or decide to do something else. When we work with clients, we use this equation to make sure that each of them has their own personalized Wealth Building Formula® and their own particular benchmarks to track. This allows them to see the effect on all of their financial decisions and if they are on track with their financial plan.

EVERYONE'S FORMULA IS DIFFERENT.

Knowing your personal Wealth Building Formula® is critical to achieving the financial independence you want within a time frame that's workable for your goals and how you wish to live now. Once you've nailed that down, the second critical part is *working* your formula. How do you work it? When you're making financial decisions, your Wealth Building Formula® is the yardstick against which you measure them.

WEALTH BUILDING FORMULA®

C × T × % Return = $$$

Investable Cash × Time × % Return = Annual Cash Flow for
Financial Independence

How does it work?

If you have to save <u>$100,000</u> per year ("C") but you actually save
<u>$125,000</u> (or more than you have to), the following can happen:

↑ C × ↓ T × ↓ % Return = ↑ $$$

T can <u>decrease,</u> *% Return* can <u>decrease,</u> or
you have <u>more</u> cash flow due to <u>increased</u> wealth.

If you have to save <u>$100,000</u> per year ("C") but actually you save
only <u>$75,000</u> (or less than you have to),
the following can happen:

↓ C × ↑ T × ↑ % Return = ↓ $$$

T can <u>increase,</u> *% Return* can <u>increase,</u> or
you have <u>less</u> cash flow due to <u>decreased</u> wealth.

The numbers represented in the equation **C × T × % Return = $$$**
are variables. A change in one of the variables on the left side of
the equation will have an effect on the right side—the cash flow for

which you are planning. A change on the right side of the equation will have an effect on one or all of the variables on the left side. Knowing what these variables are, the effects caused by changes in any one of them, and targeting and keeping track of them will allow you to make the right financial choices.

Let's look at an example: If you can save more than you target annually to "C" (the amount of wealth you need to generate cash flow), then the "T" (time) it will take to get there will be reduced. Or, you can afford to earn less "% Return," or the cash flow you are targeting could be greater. If you save less than your annual target to "C" or use money from your wealth for some purpose, then "T" will have to be increased, or you will have to raise the "% Return" to achieve your cash flow, or your cash flow will be less.

The Wealth Building Formula® serves multiple purposes. First, it guarantees that you have your own personal metrics. Your cash flow, as indicated by the dollar sign in my equation, is the key. Everyone's is different—it's what you'd need every year, inflation adjusted for the rest of your life, so that if you stopped working today or left your business today, you could live the life you want for the rest of your life.

It's critical that you know the wealth you need when you want to retire, and the rate of return you need on your wealth to maintain that financial independence, adjusted for inflation. If you know your own personal Wealth Building Formula®, you will make financial decisions that are aligned with what you want 100 percent of the time. If you save more than you have to or acquire more wealth than you need to be independent, you'll work a shorter time, or be able to take less risk with your investments, or wind up with more cash flow.

I had a client who owned a high-end jewelry store. Her profits were $550,000 a year, but in putting together her Wealth Building Formula® she realized that in order to achieve her financial goals she'd need to earn $750,000. She had the choice to leave the store the way it was, and accept that she'd have to work longer or live on less, or she could take action. She had the choice of decreasing expenses, or increasing income. How would she accomplish her goals?

She added some prestigious lines of watches to her inventory. That added some income. She also looked at opening another store. Often, people will expand their enterprises because they feel compelled to do so, but for her, it was a strategic choice based on her Wealth Building Formula®. Subsequently, her income from these actions rose to $750,000, which allowed her to reach her goals in less time.

THE BUSINESS WEALTH BUILDING FORMULA™

Whereas most people work for someone else and are dependent on a paycheck, a business owner has an advantage when it comes to building wealth. If the business is producing enough money, then they can live the lifestyle they want, pay their taxes, and put aside money in a pension plan or other accounts to build their wealth and retire—and the business itself is an additional asset that can add to their personal wealth when it's sold.

That's why, as you're running your business, you need to be sure you're taking the necessary actions to insure it has the highest value possible so that when you sell it, that wealth that you get at closing adds to your own personal wealth.

Preparing your business for sale is like preparing your home for sale. If you're going to sell the house, you're smart to put money and effort into improving its functionality and curb appeal, because that's likely to result in you getting a higher price. Owning a business is similar—you'll want to maximize your profit when you're ready to sell. What can you do to dress up your enterprise and make it as appealing as possible to a buyer?

The first thing to know is that businesses also have a Wealth Building Formula®, just as individuals do.

The Business Wealth Building Formula™ is:

$$V \times T \times G\% = \$\$\$$$

V is value—the price for which you wish to sell the business.

T is the time frame in which to sell it. Within what time frame do you want to sell your business? Five years? Ten years? This is the time frame within which you need to increase its value.

G% is growth rate. What's the annual percentage of growth rate of the business that you need to meet the value you need?

Finally, **$$$** is the cash flow, or the EBITDA, which stands for "earnings before interest, taxes, depreciation, and amortization." A multiple of EBITDA is the basis for how all businesses are valued.

This is similar to the personal Wealth Building Formula® except that, in the business formula, you're eventually going to sell the business that produces your cash flow to someone else. The way most business sales or most business valuations are structured is around what cash flow the new owner expects to get, and that determines how much they're going to pay for it.

Let's say I've got a million dollars to invest. I can put it into the market or buy a business. If I put it in the market, my expectation might be that I'd make 5 percent, or $50,000 a year. That might be less risky than owning a business, so if that's all the business is making, I'd probably pass on buying it. But let's say the business is earning $200,000. How much would I pay for that cash stream? Well, for me to earn $200,000 in the market at 5 percent, I would need $4 million. But again, there's more risk to owning a business, so I might demand a higher rate of return from the business than I would from the market. I might decide, "Whatever I invest in that, I want to earn 20 percent on my money because the money invested in a business means higher risk for me." I might be willing to spend $1 million for a business that produces $200,000 a year for me because that's a 20 percent return. So, in this case, I have valued the business at five times the bottom line (adjusted to become EBITDA). This is why focusing on your Business Wealth Building Formula® is so important for you.

As a business owner, if you need your business to earn a certain amount of profit to raise its value, there are actions you have to take to get it there. If a business has an EBITDA or earnings of only $100,000, and assuming the multiple you think you can get for your business is six, you may only get $600,000 for that business. If you need to get $6 million for your business, you've got to get the EBITDA up to $1,000,000.

Take my jewelry store owner in the earlier example. If she'd wanted to get her profits up more quickly, she could have opened a third store, or taken on more high-end lines of merchandise to close the gap between her profits and her EBITDA, and raised the value of her business for a buyer.

By the way, as in the jewelry store example, your business might have an EBITDA of $750,000. But if you are running the business like my friend did, a new owner might have to hire someone to run the stores to replace you. This might cost the new owner $500,000. Now, the store only has a profit-adjusted EBITDA of $250,000. In this case, she may have to adjust her profit to cover the cost of replacing the owner/operator.

PLANNING MAKES ALL THE DIFFERENCE—THE SOONER YOU START, THE MORE OPTIONS YOU'LL HAVE.

Most people go out into the working world without having any financial targets beyond, "Enough to pay my bills, put my kids through college, save to my 401(k), and hope I'll have enough when I retire." How much easier might it be if, instead of doing that, you asked, "How much do I really need in wealth?" and then planning your business or your personal life around that? You'd be surprised how most people would get there in the time frame they wanted, or less, if they just looked at it in the way we do when we're advising our clients.

By knowing and working the Wealth Building Formula® of your business, you're actually working your own—so that you can work less in life, get to your financial goals sooner, and/or reduce the risk in your investment portfolio. If you have more wealth, you can afford to earn less in the market and take less risk.

Most business owners have worked for someone first. They're used to having a job to cover expenses, so that when they start a business, all they're trying to do is cover their expenses. Their focus is on, "What do I need to get by?" rather than, "What do I need to live the way I want?" Most people let their careers or businesses dictate their lives, rather than running their careers in a way that will give them what they want in life. Your business is a tool: you can use it to craft the specifics of the kind of life you want for yourself, now and in the future, but that requires mindfulness and planning.

Those business owners who get what they want are most often those who consciously shape their business. The business doesn't shape them. If they see that their current business is never going to provide what they want, they either change the business, or go into another career.

> *Your business is a tool: you can use it to craft the specifics of the kind of life you want for yourself, now and in the future, but that requires mindfulness and planning.*

Sometimes this requires getting creative. My client, Bill, had a successful ceramic tile installation business for many years. But foreign competition slowly ate into his business. How could he reinvent his enterprise to gain back and add to its value? Much of the tile he manufactured was meant for bathrooms. He looked around and found a small company that manufactured glass shower doors, and he bought it out. Bill moved his business into full service bathroom installation, and in doing so he revived his business. Eventually he sold his business for a nice profit and retired.

Bill started out knowing what he wanted to achieve. My company advised him regarding personal financial planning and created both his personal and business Wealth Building Formula®. He realized he needed more cash flow, and that he'd need to get a certain figure for his business when it was time for him to sell. Knowing that end result early on made it possible for him to focus on making the kinds of necessary choices that would get him there. It's like looking across the landscape to a mountain in the distance. If the mountain is your goal, and you can keep it in sight as you drive toward it, you'll get there even if you hit some zigs and zags in the road. You may have to take a more circuitous route than you'd like, and occasionally even double back if you hit a roadblock—losing a key client or important employee, for instance, but ultimately, as long as you're focusing on the long view, you'll arrive.

NAVIGATING TOUGH TIMES IS PART OF THE JOURNEY.

There's nobody who has founded a business or who has run one for a long period of time that has not or will not hit a point where they're on the rocks and be ready to walk away. Challenges are a given in business. It's how you face them that matters. There are some people who get by it, and others who quit. The way to survive is to change how you run your business. You tweak or pivot. You create or invent something else, or take a new approach. You reinvent yourself. The important thing is keeping that end goal in sight, and being able to recalibrate your route as you're traveling. Even then, as best-seller author and entrepreneur Greg Godek described to me how he has dealt with tough cash flow periods: "Mostly by biting nails and drinking wine." Most business owners would agree with this.

I worked with two partners in a sales organization. They had a proprietary product, a tool that was very useful in a couple of different industries. Both of them had come from a sales background, and with this product they'd done very well. But eventually competition emerged for their product as alternatives appeared in the market-place, and sales were falling off.

At that particular time, they were in their mid-fifties. The two of them sat down with us and each built out their own personal Wealth

Building Formula® based on what they respectively needed in terms of supporting their lifestyles at that time and in the future. What would it require for them to achieve financial independence? Keep in mind that, when you've got partners in a business, everyone has a different Wealth Building Formula® and cash flow need, because their lives are different. They each had to independently know what they needed, and they had to make sure that their business was going to produce what they both wanted.

But at that point, the business wasn't keeping up with their needs. They had already cut costs as deeply as they could, so there were no more savings to be found. There's only so much you can cut, and you can't cut your way to prosperity. Now they had to makes some choices. Should they leave the business and go work for someone else? Or was there another line of products they could sell or develop? But this time they weren't just looking to amp up their cash flow; they had decided they needed to do everything they could to add value to their business, since both were within sight of the ages at which they wanted to retire. They chose to pivot: they discovered another company in their segment, manufacturing another kind of industrial tool, whose owner was ready to retire. They made a deal to buy that business, and were able to successfully rejuvenate their business by doing so.

It's critical to look ahead as you're planning your business's future. Where will you be in five years? Ten years? Will there still be a demand for what you're selling, or is it likely to be replaced or outmoded? If you think your product is still going to be in demand, then it's a matter of expanding your clientele or sales and watching costs. If you think that in the future your market is at peril, you may have to change markets or you may have to do something that's going to augment your business to buffer you against that shift in the market, as well as making sure that you're running your business in the most cost-efficient manner.

IF YOU'RE SICK AND TIRED OF WHAT YOU DO, DO SOMETHING ELSE.

I've talked a little in previous chapters about how important it is to our happiness and satisfaction in life that we love what we do for a living, and nowhere is that more true than it is for a business owner. The fact is that most business owners work far harder than employees generally do. If you're putting in years of long hours working and strategizing and worrying over something, it had better give you joy. If you can get in a business that you really love, one where you wake up every day and you can't wait to get to work, and you can earn the money you need to live the life you want, pay your taxes, and put aside the money to eventually retire, or sell the business at a nice price in your retirement, that's ideal.

That's not how it works for most people. They normally get in a business they have the best talent for, or one they may have inherited from a relation. Maybe they get into a particular business because, when they got out of school, that was the industry in which they got their first couple of jobs, so their path was set. Another scenario might be they worked for someone. One day the owner wanted to sell, and they bought it, because it seemed like a good enough life. But in any of these situations, if you reach the critical point where your business isn't fulfilling either your personal or your financial needs, it may be time to reinvent yourself.

Keep in mind, it's like anything in life—you can be at the mercy of your business or career, or you can choose to control your business or career. If you're in a situation where you don't like your business or what you're doing, you can change it. If you feel like you're on a treadmill, you're not alone: millions of business owners and employees alike feel that way. To me, that's no way to live your life. No matter what excuses you make, you don't have to keep working this way.

> *You can be at the mercy of your business or career, or you can choose to control your business or career.*

What happens when a business owner is unhappy? Their work is not as inspiring. It's not as efficient or as effective, and they do poorly in their businesses. That failure to reach their financial goals only compounds their unhappiness. Barry Moltz is an author and speaker in small business and entrepreneurship, and is a member of the Entrepreneurship Hall of Fame. If you feel that you are "stuck" in your business, you may want to read his book, *How to Get Unstuck*. Barry makes it clear he loves the business of making small businesses more successful. If you're on that treadmill, start actively exploring what options you have to get off of it.

I knew a lawyer who was absolutely miserable in his career—a career that he'd worked years to get, and one in which he was very talented. He was a senior partner at a specialty law firm, and financially was doing very well, but he had reached the point at which he felt that financial security just wasn't a reasonable trade for the quality of life he wanted to have. It got to where he was so unhappy it affected his marriage and his relationship with his children because he was just miserable all the time. And while he had a great talent for what he did, it did eventually started to affect his work.

It was at this juncture in his life that I was working with him and his spouse, helping them to set their financial house in order. He confided his dilemma to me, but said that he couldn't see any alternative to just staying where he was until he was wealthy enough to retire. This was all he knew. I encouraged him to think creatively about what other options might be open to him, something that utilized his expertise without chaining him to work in the field in which he was so unhappy. He decided to do just that, and quit the practice of law to start a new business selling legal software and supplies to law firms. It was a perfect fit; he knew what law offices needed to run, and tailored his firm to cater to their needs. He had a wide list of acquaintances in that world, and leveraged those contacts to get his first customers. Now he's happier as a successful businessman, and is well on his way to the financial independence he wants when he's ready to sell his company. Even though there's stress in any business, he far preferred the stresses of running his own company to those he'd experienced as a partner in a law firm. He enjoyed the kinds of personal interactions he had; he got up every morning looking forward to going to work.

I can vouch for the wisdom of making that leap from my own experience. Thirty-five years ago, I had a great career in the tax department at Ernst & Young in New York City, and I continued that career at Merck & Company, Inc. I had seniority and great responsibilities and I enjoyed both companies. It's likely that, had I stayed, I would have risen to the ranks of senior management. But it wasn't for me. I wanted to run my own company. And while I recognized that starting a business was an inherently risky proposition, I also saw that being an employee isn't necessarily any more secure. Companies go broke, reorganize, and even good people get laid off. Michael Hauge, a successful Hollywood story and script consultant, author, and lecturer who works with writers and filmmakers on their screenplays, novels, movies, and television projects started his company for some of the same reasons: "I never liked working for a boss. I've enjoyed being on my own, working with clients I want and making my own schedule."[12]

I was willing to take a risk to live my life in the way I wished, and I'm very glad I got off that treadmill when I did. And while I have experienced the ups and downs all business owners experience, I have never regretted it. As the old adage says, "Know thyself," and live accordingly.

Chapter 5 Takeaways

- Whether we're talking about your personal financial goals, or your goals for your business, the Wealth Building Formula® gives you the knowledge you need to make the right decisions 100 percent of the time, every step of the way.

- There is a personal Wealth Building Formula® and a Business Wealth Building Formula™, and you need to know them and how to work them both.

- When you're making financial decisions, your Wealth Building Formula® is the yardstick against which you measure them.

---

12   Michael Hauge, interview with author.

CHAPTER SIX

THE POWER OF COMPOUNDING

"Compound Interest is the eighth wonder of the world."
—Albert Einstein

Alex approached me after my speech to a group of Houston business owners on how to find more cash flow in a business. A senior partner in a law firm, Alex told me he was intrigued by what I'd said about how everyday decisions business owners made could significantly impact their bottom line. His firm was grossing $3 million, but the firm was not making much money. He and his partners had just been discussing how they might more effectively structure their cash flow, and he wanted to arrange a phone consultation with me. I agreed, and he sent me the firm's financial statements to review. When we got on the phone, I told him he could probably double or triple the bottom line of the practice.

After a brief review, I told him, "First, you need to restructure your debt for a longer term: you're paying it off too quickly. Second, I looked at billing rates in your area for comparable firms, and yours are lower than they should be. Lastly, your accounts receivable policies are weak and your clerk is not staying on top of collections. This is costing you cash flow."

By making those few changes in how they ran their business, they easily added 50 percent to the bottom line. He and another one of the senior partners hired me to be their wealth advisors, and this year they're on track to pull down $7 million. That doesn't mean they had to quadruple their working hours or work harder. It's just that now they were working for the business rather than working in the business. And because of that, now they will have choices in life that weren't available to them before, especially about how long they'll have to work and the kind of lifestyle they can enjoy in retirement. But what does any of this have to do with compounding? Having this extra cash flow and saving it allowed them to take full advantage of compounding to achieve their wealth goals faster, and in fact have more wealth. And since they had more wealth, they didn't have to risk as much in the market to make a high return for the cash flow they needed.

These were smart people, but I still had to sit down with them and explain how compounding works and why it makes such a critical difference in how quickly you accumulate wealth. If you don't understand basic financial principles, it can be hard to grasp how important compounding is.

If you're like most busy business owners, you're thinking, "Ugh, compounding—this sounds so boring, so technical. Why do I need to know this stuff? Just let me get out there and sell. Let me run my business."

Okay, I'll explain. Let's look into your future, thirty years from now. You have your business, and you're getting ready to retire. You wish you could leave it as a legacy to your heirs, but you have to sell it because you don't have enough put away on which to retire comfortably. It's no comfort to consider at this point that, had you made better business decisions over the last thirty years—or even in the last ten years—you would have more options in life. Maybe you could have passed it to the next generation, or given it to others in the firm. You'd have that luxury if you'd taken the time to understand the power of compounding. Compounding gives you these kinds of choices, and if you can't be bothered to learn about it here, you're effectively sentencing yourself to having fewer choices in your future.

On the other hand, if you take the time to understand compounding and to start using it sooner rather than later, you will almost certainly have more cash flow in the future. You may be able to retire earlier, and with a better lifestyle. And you might be able to pass that business into which you've poured so much sweat equity and love to your children.

Is compounding beginning to sound more interesting?

WHY IS COMPOUNDING TOUGH TO GRASP?

Human beings are linear thinkers. We don't think in terms of compounding, which is why we need calculators to figure out things like mortgage payments. Money growth doesn't work in a linear fashion; it compounds in a geometric way. Most people don't really understand the power of compounding, and their lack of that knowledge hinders their ability to make better financial choices. People may be familiar with the general concept of compounding on some level, but usually not with any real clarity or comprehension, and they simply don't believe it even when it's explained to them.

How does compounding work? One good analogy is to think of how bacteria grow in Petri dishes. A bacterial colony starts out slowly; one cell becomes two, which become four, and so on. But at a certain point the doubling really takes off, and it seems to explode. Now you're talking about much larger numbers being created in the same span of time. This is sort of how compounding works: It starts slowly. It takes time. But if you're patient and stay on course, it gets to a point where it grows at a much more rapid pace. Remember: as a business owner, your ultimate goal is to pay yourself the amount that you need to the live the life you want, to pay your taxes, and to put money aside toward your financial independence. Compounding can make that happen faster.

Remember: as a business owner, your ultimate goal is to pay yourself the amount that you need to the live the life you want, to pay your taxes, and to put money aside toward your financial independence. Compounding can make that happen faster.

Take a look at the chart I've included here, which compares the relative gains made by the Savvy Business Owner versus the Slow Business Owner, to better understand the gains compounding can bring.

THE POWER OF COMPOUNDING
SAVE NOW VERSUS LATER

Year	Savvy Business Owner! Contribution	Wealth	Slow Business Owner Contribution	Wealth
1	$10,000	$10,700	$0	$0
2	$10,000	22,149	0	0
3	$10,000	34,399	0	0
4	$10,000	47,507	0	0
5	$10,000	61,533	0	0
6	$10,000	76,540	0	0
7	$10,000	92,598	0	0
8	$10,000	109,780	0	0
9	$10,000	128,164	0	0
10	$10,000	147,836	0	0
11	$10,000	168,885	10,000	10,700
12	$10,000	191,406	10,000	22,149
13	$10,000	215,505	10,000	34,399
14	$10,000	241,290	10,000	47,507
15	$10,000	268,881	10,000	61,533
16	$10,000	298,402	10,000	76,540
17	$10,000	329,990	10,000	92,598
18	$10,000	363,790	10,000	109,780
19	$10,000	399,955	10,000	128,164
20	$10,000	438,652	10,000	147,836
21	$10,000	480,057	10,000	168,885
22	$10,000	524,361	10,000	191,406
23	$10,000	571,767	10,000	215,505
24	$10,000	622,490	10,000	241,290
25	$10,000	676,765	10,000	268,881
26	$10,000	734,838	10,000	298,402
27	$10,000	796,977	10,000	329,990
28	$10,000	863,465	10,000	363,790
29	$10,000	934,608	10,000	399,955
30	$10,000	1,010,730	10,000	438,652
31	$10,000	1,092,182	10,000	480,057
32	$10,000	1,179,334	10,000	524,361
33	$10,000	1,272,588	10,000	571,767
34	$10,000	1,372,369	10,000	622,490
35	$10,000	1,479,135	10,000	676,765
36	$10,000	1,593,374	10,000	734,838
37	$10,000	1,715,610	10,000	796,977
38	$10,000	1,846,403	10,000	863,465
39	$10,000	1,986,351	10,000	934,608
40	$10,000	2,136,096	10,000	1,010,730
41	$10,000	2,296,322	10,000	1,092,182
42	$10,000	2,467,765	10,000	1,179,334
43	$10,000	$2,651,209	10,000	$1,272,588
Total Contributions	$430,000		$330,000	

7% assumed rate of return

This first illustration shows the Savvy Owner saving $10,000 per year from year one. The Slow Owner skips the first ten years, maybe paying off debt, and then saves starting in year eleven. The Savvy Owner saved a bit more over the years, but ends more with more than twice what the Slow Owner has ended up with.

Now suppose the Savvy Owner restructures their debt so that they're paying over a longer term, freeing up an extra $100,000 per year in cash flow instead of $10,000. She decides to put that aside in savings.

The Slow Owner gets that same $100,000, but uses it to pay down debt over ten years. In the eleventh year, he begins putting that annual $100,000 into savings, just like the Savvy Owner.

Now look at how dramatically their results differ. In forty-three years of steadily saving $100,000 per year, the Savvy Owner has put in a total of $4.3 million—but has amassed over $26.5 million.

The Slow Owner put away $3.3 million over thirty-three years—only ten fewer years than the Savvy Owner, but has amassed only $12,725,876.00, less than half of what the savvy business owner has. How? Time. Time is the factor that allows compounding to work its magic.

Like the Slow Owner, many people have a knee-jerk aversion to debt, and do their best to pay it off as quickly as possible. Here's a recent example: I met with a business owner who had bought some expensive manufacturing equipment in the past year. He'd made the choice to finance this purchase over three years rather than over a longer period, so he had to come up with more money to pay it off quicker. That ate up cash to the tune of an extra $100,000 per year. That's not the smart financial choice; that $100,000 a year could have been earning money and compounding for him, so he was effectively losing wealth because of that decision.

THE POWER OF COMPOUNDING
SAVE NOW VERSUS LATER

Year	Savvy Business Owner! Contribution	Wealth	Slow Business Owner Contribution	Wealth
1	$100,000	$107,000	$0	$0
2	$100,000	221,490	0	0
3	$100,000	343,994	0	0
4	$100,000	475,074	0	0
5	$100,000	615,329	0	0
6	$100,000	765,402	0	0
7	$100,000	925,980	0	0
8	$100,000	1,097,799	0	0
9	$100,000	1,281,645	0	0
10	$100,000	1,478,360	0	0
11	$100,000	1,688,845	100,000	107,000
12	$100,000	1,914,064	100,000	221,490
13	$100,000	2,155,049	100,000	343,994
14	$100,000	2,412,902	100,000	475,074
15	$100,000	2,688,805	100,000	615,329
16	$100,000	2,984,022	100,000	765,402
17	$100,000	3,299,903	100,000	925,980
18	$100,000	3,637,896	100,000	1,097,799
19	$100,000	3,999,549	100,000	1,281,645
20	$100,000	4,386,518	100,000	1,478,360
21	$100,000	4,800,574	100,000	1,688,845
22	$100,000	5,243,614	100,000	1,914,064
23	$100,000	5,717,667	100,000	2,155,049
24	$100,000	6,224,904	100,000	2,412,902
25	$100,000	6,767,647	100,000	2,688,805
26	$100,000	7,348,382	100,000	2,984,022
27	$100,000	7,969,769	100,000	3,299,903
28	$100,000	8,634,653	100,000	3,637,896
29	$100,000	9,346,079	100,000	3,999,549
30	$100,000	10,107,304	100,000	4,386,518
31	$100,000	10,921,815	100,000	4,800,574
32	$100,000	11,793,343	100,000	5,243,614
33	$100,000	12,725,876	100,000	5,717,667
34	$100,000	13,723,688	100,000	6,224,904
35	$100,000	14,791,346	100,000	6,767,647
36	$100,000	15,933,740	100,000	7,348,382
37	$100,000	17,156,102	100,000	7,969,769
38	$100,000	18,464,029	100,000	8,634,653
39	$100,000	19,863,511	100,000	9,346,079
40	$100,000	21,360,957	100,000	10,107,304
41	$100,000	22,963,224	100,000	10,921,815
42	$100,000	24,677,650	100,000	11,793,343
43	$100,000	$26,512,085	100,000	$12,725,876
Total Contributions	$4,300,000		$3,300,000	

7% assumed rate of return

Even the most intelligent people have a tough time with compounding. I met recently with a business owner who's about forty-five, and told him, "Look, I can add another $100,000 or $200,000 a year to your income by making changes in how you handle your debt and cash flow. By the time you are sixty-five, it's going to be worth $5 million."

He looked startled; "I don't see how! $100,000 a year over fifteen years only comes to 1.5 million." I had to walk him through the chart I've included here to make the power of compounding clear to him. The lesson is clear: it takes you longer to create wealth if you don't take advantage of compounding. If you save later, you have to save longer and work harder to end up with less than the person who saves and takes advantage of compounding sooner.

DO YOUR PART, AND COMPOUNDING WILL DO ITS PART.

Compounding is actually pretty amazing—if you stick to your plan. If you have a plan in mind over ten, twenty, thirty, or forty years, compounding works in a special way we call "geometric compounding."

Let's say that a person starting from zero today has a twenty-five-year wealth goal to be independent and calculates the amount of wealth needed to accomplish that (using the Wealth Building Formula®). There is going to be an amount that person must save each year at an assumed rate of return to reach that goal. The key is to get to geometric compounding. Geometric compounding works in a way that's very predictable—you can calculate it very easily—but because compounding starts off slowly and only gains a lot of steam way down the line, it can discourage you from saving or making the proper financial choice.

What do I mean by that? While compounding begins when you first start to save, the real power of compounding occurs in the later stage of your wealth building. If you diligently save what you are supposed to save annually, then you will reach geometric compounding about two-thirds of the way through the time frame of your financial plan. At this point, if you look at what you have accrued in wealth, you will see that you have about one-third of what you need to be financially independent.

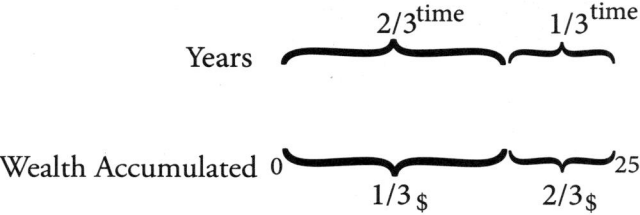

Chances are you'll begin to lose faith in compounding at that point. How in the world can you make up two-thirds of your financial goal when you've only got one third of the allotted time in which to accomplish that? People can fall off the saving wagon, or just decide, "To heck with it—I'm never going to hit my goal, so I might as well just enjoy the money now." Others will look at shifting their assets to higher-risk investments or to money managers that "guarantee" high returns (remember Bernie Madoff?). But hang in there, because if you have saved faithfully, the "magic" of compounding occurs in the last one-third of the time, generating two-thirds of the returns.

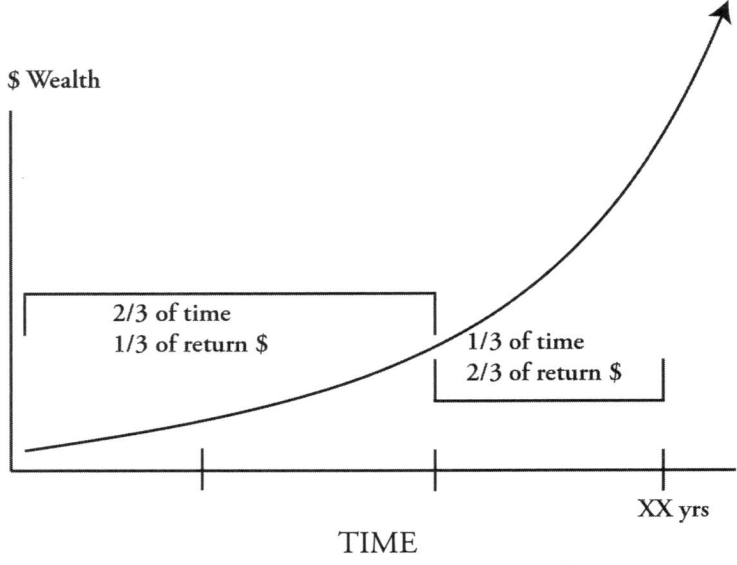

Even though you're two-thirds through your allotted time and see that you've only saved a third of what you need, stick with it, because the magic of what we call the "geometric jump" happens in that last third of your financial plan. If I were to draw a line showing the progress of geometric compounding, the line would be relatively flat from year zero to about year sixteen or seventeen, and then it would go up geometrically. If you stick with the plan and keep saving, it's during that last third that you actually make up more than two-thirds of the wealth that you need to achieve your goals. (See the compounding and "Geometric Jump" charts above.)

It really, really works—as long as you stay on board and work your plan.

When I show clients the Power of Compounding charts I've included previously, they'll often look at it, shrug, and say, "Al, I'm fifty years old. I may not have forty-three years!"

I say, "Yes, that may be true. But you know what? You're not starting from zero like the illustration. You've already accumulated wealth, and the choices you make over the next ten, twenty, or thirty years are going to decide how much more wealth and how much more cash flow you will have in the future, versus now. You can be slow and have less, or you can be savvy and have more."

As you can see, adding that $100,000 per year to savings over a longer period of time maximizes the power of compounding—and when you start is critically important. Two people putting in the same amount of money in different time frames will have dramatically different results.

What I try to impress upon people is the decisions you're making today, especially over the next ten years, will have a profound impact for the next ten, twenty, or thirty years beyond that. If you're a business owner today, and you're fifty years old and clearly behind in your savings, if you take corrective actions today, the next ten years will have a profound effect on how you live, and how hard you work, for the rest of your life.

WHAT HAPPENS IF YOU DON'T USE COMPOUNDING TO BUILD YOUR WEALTH?

If you don't understand the principles of compounding, you're always going to be surprised when you see numbers, and you may be making decisions that don't allow you to maximize the power of compounding.

By not understanding the power of compounding, by not making the best financial decisions throughout the life of the company, by the time you're thinking of retiring, you may not have a choice about it. You may wish that you could give your business to your heirs but you can't, and your heirs may not be able to afford to pay for it. Thus, not making the proper financial decisions during the course of your career takes options out of your hands. It takes choices away from you.

If you don't use compounding to build your wealth, you may be tempted to put your profits other places—into paying down debt, or other kinds of less-certain investments. You're making choices, but not necessarily good ones. And those will impact the kinds of choices you get to make down the line. I was able to save the partners in that firm I described earlier from having to work longer and harder than they wanted to in life, because I showed them they could make a better choice.

Most people go into work just to work the day they put in their businesses. They don't spend part of that day saying, "What do I need this business to produce for me, and how do I get there?"

This book is here to show you that the choices you make every day—the course corrections and options you chose or reject—are in your hands. It's like taking care of your physical health. If you work regularly at getting fit every day over a period of years, you'll build a foundation of solid strength and health that will sustain you into your old age. You'll feel better than those who didn't exercise do. Just like physical fitness, financial fitness isn't something you can crunch into a short time frame and hope to see long-term results. There are no "seven minute abs" in wealth-building, as much as we might wish there were.

Using the power of compounding is like adopting a routine of regular exercise—the results may take a long time to show up, and you might get frustrated at what seems like slow progress. But if you stick with it, you'll see real rewards in the future when you need them most, and your range of choices in life will be much greater.

Chapter 6 Takeaways

- If you take the time to understand compounding and to start using it sooner rather than later, you will almost certainly have more wealth and cash flow in the future.

- Compounding starts slowly. It takes time. But if you're patient and stay on course, you will harness its power.

- If you save later, you have to save longer and work harder to end up with less than the person who saves and takes advantage of compounding sooner.

- You might get frustrated at what seems like slow progress, but if you stick with it, your range of choices in life will be much greater.

CHAPTER SEVEN

THE TAX SAVINGS SAVINGS EFFECT: A KEY TO MAKING GREAT BUSINESS DECISIONS

"The politicians say 'we' can't afford a tax cut.
Maybe we can't afford the politicians."
—Steve Forbes

U nderstanding the Tax Savings Savings Effect can help make the difference between your company's success or failure. It's the margin between your company being worth X dollars or half that, the difference between your company having enough cash flow to expand or not. Being aware of it is part of holding that CFO mind-set—keeping your company's targets in view, and making the choices that will enable you to hit them.

Were you ever unpleasantly surprised by an eleventh-hour call from your accountant as April 15 neared, informing you that you owed far more in taxes than you'd planned for? If sufficient cash wasn't put aside to cover those taxes, you may find your business in a hole—or sucked down the drain. Yet for most smaller and medium-sized businesses and organizations, tax planning consists of giving the accountant their information in February or March, then getting the return back from the accountant at the last minute in April. That's not proper tax planning, that's roulette.

How can you properly plan for tax time, and what decisions should play into that planning? First of all, get time on your side. Good tax planning doesn't happen in March, it should occur throughout the year, with more intense reviews and revisions in the third and fourth quarters. By the end of the current year, you should already know what your tax return looks like. At each of these review points, you and your accountant must sit down and go through your expenses and the cash flow coming in, and plan for whatever capital expenditures you want to make. For instance, if you're in the fourth quarter and you're planning on expanding or buying new equipment in January, you're likely to find it's smarter from a tax-planning standpoint to make that purchase in December. You may also find that there are other expenses you're better off paying out in December before the year's end, such as employee bonuses, purchasing supplies, or charitable contributions. Most businesses don't take this into consideration, which means that the $50,000 or $100,000 they could have saved in taxes, they now have to pay. Obviously this can impair a company's growth, force cutbacks and layoffs, or even shutter it.

Knowing how taxes work is fundamental to understanding how to make the Tax Savings Savings Effect work for you. Most people think, "My tax bracket is 40 percent. Whatever I'm either spending or earning, that's what I'll have to pay." But it's not necessarily true, and the effect will be higher or lower based on how you're going to spend those earnings. Making the right choices is key to managing your cash flow. Those who understand tax savings will prosper, and those who don't will pay.

Note the following illustration of the Tax Savings Savings Effect.

TAX SAVINGS SAVINGS EFFECT
(OR HOW TO TURN $30,000 INTO $50,000 WITHOUT WORKING HARDER)

$30,000 × 40%	=	$12,000.00
12,000 × 40%	=	4,800.00
4,800 × 40%	=	1,920.00
1,920 × 40%	=	768.00
768 × 40%	=	307.00
307 × 40%	=	123.00
123 × 40%	=	49.00
49 × 40%	=	20.00
20 × 40%	=	8.00
8 × 40%	=	3.00
3 × 40%	=	1.00
1 × 40%	=	.40
.40 × 40%	=	.16

Totals (rounded up) $50,000 × 40% = $20,000

So, to save $30,000 (non tax sheltered), you must earn $50,000 and pay $20,000 in income taxes. Having to earn $50,000 to net after tax to $30,000 makes sense since 40% of $50,000 equals taxes of $20,000.

If you can shelter $30,000 (in something like a pension plan), you save income taxes. If you shelter the income tax savings, you save more. If you keep on doing this, you can save $50,000 rather then just the $30,000. Remember the Power of Compounding? You can get to your goals sooner, work less years, or just have more wealth just by knowing how to use the Tax Savings Savings Effect. By the way, if you can only save $300 to begin with, you can save $500 this way. Or $5,000 if you can save $3,000. Get the point?

I met recently with a client who has a healthy medium-sized business, and who wanted to explore the most effective ways to put money into retirement funds for himself and his employees. We showed him that, as the majority owner and the CEO, while he has a 401(k), he could establish a cash balance pension plan and contribute $600,000 for him and his key people. He had thirty employees, and for the support staff, they would have to put away $100,000. That's a total of $700,000, His business is in New York City, and they're in the 50 percent-plus tax bracket for local, state, and federal taxes. By contributing this $700,000 to a pension plan, they'll lower their taxes by more than $350,000. The bad news is that they've been in business a long time, and could have done this every year, but they hadn't been thinking like CFOs.

MAKE THE GOVERNMENT HELP YOU CREATE CASH FLOW.

Here's an example of how smarter planning might work for your business: Right now, the law says that if you spend up to $1 million for equipment, you might be able to expense it all in one year rather than over many years. Let's say it's November or December, and you're planning a big expansion for next year for which you need to purchase equipment. You're planning to spend that $500,000 in the first quarter of the coming year, because your cash flow is a little tight right now and that's when you anticipate a lot of cash will come in from receivables. Sounds sensible, given the cash crunch you're in, but is it? No, because you're throwing away valuable cash flow from tax savings that you could use now!

Instead, why not go to the bank and get a short-term loan to buy the equipment before the end of the year? Then you get the tax credits now! Alternately, if you have enough credit to cover that $500,000, why don't you use that to buy the equipment, then when the cash comes in January or February, just pay off the liability? I'd bet you could also negotiate a better price from the vendor too, because they want their sales numbers for the year to be good. That gives you a hefty $500,000 tax deduction for this year, and that saves you serious money.

Even smaller businesses can use this kind of planning. Let's say you need $25,000 of equipment, but can't gather the cash to make the purchase by the end of the year. Do you have a credit card with a $25,000 line of credit available to you? If so, use it to pay for the equipment before the end of the year, and pay off that debt in the new year, maybe by the end of January when your cash flow is better. You can pick up valuable cash flow this way.

Similarly, you may be planning to pay your employees their bonuses at the end of January because you want to be clear about where you stand financially before you do. But if you know you've had a good year, it's better to approximate those bonuses based on the figures you've been tracking and pay them *before* the end of the year, so you can claim that as a deduction.

BE THE SQUEAKY WHEEL WITH YOUR ACCOUNTANT.

This kind of strategizing is the essence of the CFO mind-set: even if your business isn't big enough to have a chief financial officer, you should be meeting with your accountant or CPA throughout the year, listening to their ideas about maximizing tax savings ahead of the year's end, and making the decisions that will benefit your fiscal health and save you money. If they do not have the time or ideas when you meet with them, it may be time to get a new accountant.

Keep in mind as your business grows, everyone at your company is busy taking care of customers or clients, so that there may be no one person charged solely with taking care of the business's financial interests. That's what a CFO does, but if you can't afford a full-time CFO, consider appointing someone to handle that job part time as part of their current position until you get a full-time person. I talked in another chapter about the importance of having a championship team in your firm, as well as outside it, to help you look for these opportunities—great hires in positions like these pay for themselves.

SMALL MONETARY CHOICES CAN MAKE A BIG WEALTH DIFFERENCE.

The key to finding more cash flow, especially concerning income taxes, is realizing that every choice you make around money in your business can and will have a tax effect (whether that's what to buy or when to buy it, when and how to fund pensions or pay bonuses, and when to dip into your cash versus when to use credit to make a business purchase or to expand). If you're not aware how much you might potentially save or have to hand over to the IRS because of the timing of those decisions, chances are very good you're paying much more in taxes than you need to.

These principles also extend to single-person enterprises. According to government statistics, nearly twenty-three million enterprises in the U.S. are one-person operations. A surprising number of these one-person businesses gross at least $1 million[13].

Are you a CEO about to retire? Maybe you will opt to become a consultant or to serve on the boards of other companies. If you plan properly, you can shelter all of your income from these activities. Many other single-person businesses can do the same.

Mary was one person who falls into this demographic. She is a very successful author, writer, and speaker. Last year on April 10 she was stunned to learn from her accountant that she owed $75,000 in taxes after a great year. Unfortunately for her she'd waited until the last minute to give her information to the accountant, and simply didn't have the money in reserve to pay the taxes she owed.

This happens so often to individuals and businesses alike; it's a story I've heard many times. At one point, we had clients who came to us not having filed their taxes for several years, because they'd had problems with their previous accountants and kept putting it off. One had a fairly big enterprise with some foreign-based subsidiaries as well as a US presence. We suspected that they'd actually understated the number of years in which they hadn't filed properly. In looking at their prior tax returns we discovered about $16 million in tax credits and losses that they could have claimed against their income over the previous seven years, but didn't.

---

13   Small Business Association, "Advocacy: The Voice of Small business in Government," September 2012, https://www.sba.gov/sites/default/files/FAQ_Sept_2012.pdf.

Now, don't get carried away by size of the numbers; it's all relative. Maybe saving $10,000 would mean a lot. Just know this cash flow is out there. In this case, they could carry those credits forward to subsequent years, but they certainly provided an object lesson in just how badly things can go awry when you're not paying attention. And when your team doesn't include a championship-level tax accountant, as theirs should have had, or when you consistently put off dealing with things, that won't take care of themselves.

A not-so-good tax accountant will cost you more—as is illustrated by the experience of another company, a small business whose owners came to see us recently. They'd had a licensing agreement with a foreign company for about $500,000 a year for a product they produced, all of which they received in one year. The payment was a lot less in the second year, and they suffered some other losses estimated at $70,000. The following year they were down half a million, and that's when they came to us.

We went over their returns and suggested, "Why don't you use the loss you had last year against the income two years ago?" They'd actually already filed the return, and we had to go back and amend it. They could have taken the $70,000 in losses against the income two years ago and created a refund of $35,000, but their accountant had missed it.

Don't get me wrong: there are a lot of great CPAs and accountants out there. But, too often, accounting firms don't take the time to tax plan for their clients in advance, or they don't review previous tax records and returns as they should. All they do is take the information that you give them, feed it into the software and pop out a return. If you don't take the time to sit with your accountant and help them to understand your business, valuable deductions can be lost. Demand that they make time to meet and review this with you. If they don't have the time, replace them!

As another example, we're working now with a Midwestern law firm whose senior partners were about to sell their interest in the practice. It's a specialty practice, worth upward of $4 million. Initially they brought us in as wealth advisors to review the recommendations their accountants had made. In reviewing their tax returns, we found a lot of missed opportunities for cash flow/tax savings. For instance, at least two-thirds of their taxable gain could have been classified as capital gains rather than ordinary income, saving them literally hundreds of thousands of dollars in taxes. Of course, their accountant had access to the same information we were given, but again, he may have been just too busy to really look at the situation. Like most accountants, he saw his job as simply feeding what they told him into a computer program and handing them whatever it spat out.

Part of having that CFO mind-set is to make sure the tax people you're dealing with take the time they need to understand how your business is conducted. They've got to be critical and creative thinkers, able to game out various scenarios to help you to take full advantage of the Tax Savings Savings Effect.

Remember: those who bring the best team on board will reap the benefits of increased cash flow, and will prosper. Those who don't will see their cash flow flowing the wrong direction away from them to the IRS, state, and local governments. As a business leader or entrepreneur, you're not required to understand the intricacies of tax law, but you'd be wise to retain someone who

Remember: those who bring the best team on board will reap the benefits of increased cash flow, and will prosper.

does. That will help guarantee that you'll have the wealth you need to grow your business and to prosper, now and in the future.

Chapter 7 Takeaways

- Understanding the Tax Savings Savings Effect can help make the difference between your company's success, or its failure.

- Good tax planning doesn't happen after January 1, it should be done throughout the year before.

- Small decisions can have a big impact on your fiscal health.

- Meet with your accountant or CPA and demand proactive ideas for saving tax dollars.

CHAPTER EIGHT

FINDING MORE CASH FLOW IN YOUR BUSINESS

"Happy are those who dream dreams and are ready to pay the price to make them come true."
—Leon J. Suenens

C ash flow: the lifeblood of your business. It doesn't matter how many orders you get, or how much product or services you're selling on paper, if cash flow into the business isn't keeping up with and surpassing the cash going out, you're going to wind up locking your doors for good sooner or later.

For some business owners strapped for cash, the only solution that presents itself to them seems to be, "Sell more!" But you can run yourself and your people ragged trying to outrun cash outflow, and still come out behind. What's the solution? Again, it requires that you adopt that CFO mind-set: setting clear targets, using multiple success drivers, finding cash in places you might not have thought to look, making well-informed decisions, and keeping close track of where the money is going.

TRACKING YOUR CASH FLOW

Let's talk about tracking your cash flow first, because your chances of finding the cash you need are diminished if you're not doing this right. You've got to have budgets and targets, as well as a clear view of how closely you're adhering to those. That requires producing a *profit and loss statement* or what I call a *breakeven statement* at least once a month, and preferably twice. I always suggest that my clients run their profit and loss statement on both the fifteenth and the last day of each month.

Once you've got that in hand, the next step is to review all your revenue lines and all your expense lines. Business builder, keynote speaker, and author of *Orgasmic Leadership*, Rachel Braun Scherl, insists that you should, "Constantly evaluate opportunities to find revenue and cut costs. Line Items that seem necessary might not be on a closer look." If your operation is larger and you have someone assisting you, you can have someone go through these first and highlight the issues before your review. If anything is off by either a certain absolute dollar amount or a pre-determined percentage in terms of your profit and loss, your budgeting, or your projections, make sure those discrepancies are noted and explained. Scherl adds, "If you don't understand the numbers of your business, hire someone to teach you. You don't have to be an accountant, financial analyst, or mathematical whiz. But if you don't understand the fundamentals, you will be hard pressed to manage your cash flow."[14]

---

14   Rachel Braun Scherl, interview with author.

In my company, when our manager of finance and operations submits the profit and loss statement to me, he's already reviewed it and highlighted those areas of discrepancy, and can explain them to me. For instance, an expense that was higher than anticipated, but will be within the budget next month. If you have a management team or partners in your business, they should all be getting this statement. It's a good thing to have multiple sets of eyes reviewing it, and getting input on what needs to be done to resolve any problems that it reveals, whether that's an unexpected expense or lower-than-anticipated revenue. And don't let this process intimidate you. While I realize that none of us jump out of bed in the morning excited about reviewing our profit and loss statements, you'll be pleasantly surprised at how quickly you'll become adept at it and how quickly the process becomes part of your business's routine.

The next report you need is a *cash flow projection*, which is different than a profit and loss statement (P&L): A P&L simply tells you what's gone out and what's come in. But other items that don't show up on a profit and loss statement—for instance, when you pay off a loan, buy new equipment, or have other necessary expenses—can put you out of business, too. A firm has to invest in itself as it's growing, has to spend money on furniture, fixtures and equipment and other necessities, but if they're spending cash flow before it's actually in hand, even a very profitable-on-paper company will find itself out of business.

Your cash projection clarifies what is actually coming in, versus what expenses you have going out so that you know what you've actually got on hand. As with your profit and loss statement, your cash flow statement should be done on the fifteenth and the final day of each month. Between these two documents, you'll have a very clear picture of your company's fiscal health and what you need to do to improve it. You'll see whether the business is performing as predicted. If not, you'll have to find extra cash flow or profitability to make up for any shortfalls.

In addition to generating these two reports twice a month, you should be meeting with your management team or the key people on that team once a month, not only to go through the reports, but also to review what I call your dashboard: your vital factors, the important indicators or benchmarks for your business. Are you making your cash flow projections? If not, then why not?

Well-run companies follow these guidelines, no matter the size. If their cash flow isn't where it needs to be, they take action to correct that, whether that means laying off employees, cutting expenses or pushing sales.

FINDING MORE CASH FLOW

How can you find more cash flow in your business? Depending on the size of your operation, one action is to prioritize or grade your staff at least annually. My management team and I get together once a year, if not twice a year, and we rank all of our staff with grades of letters A, B, or C. Those who fall into the C category should be let go. Why? Getting rid of your C-players is a money-saving move, because a bad employee probably costs you money. In their book *Who: A Method for Hiring*, authors Geoff Smart and Randy Street estimate that a C-player can cost a company the equivalent of three times their salary per year. Thus, if you're looking for cash flow or multiple drivers of success to make sure you're driving profitability, it pays to get rid of your C-players.

At my company, we play a game that I've taught to many of my clients, and I urge you to institute it in your own business. It's called the "finding money savings" game. How it works is quite simple: Every member of my management team is tasked with coming up with a way to save at least $250 for the company, and present it at our monthly meeting. It may sound small, or even silly, but you'd be amazed at what they come up with—oftentimes ideas that save much more than that. As an example, our chief investment officer renegotiated our contract with a service vendor from whom we were buying research, and was able to get them to lower their fees by about $60,000 annually. It's not uncommon with people to come to the meeting with ideas on how to reap $500, $1,000, or $2,000 in savings annually.

So often these kinds of significant savings are right under our noses. For instance, we often send clients flowers or gifts when they're celebrating a special occasion or when they're under the weather. A member of the executive team came up with the idea of using the company's accumulated air miles or credit card points to pay for these gifts. Again, that may sound insignificant, but we were able to save $10,000 a year.

When our firm's division managers have their monthly meetings with their staff, they play the $50 game, in which staff members are encouraged to look for savings of $50 per month. They have a smaller target than management. One simple idea that came out of this was just setting our copy machines' default printing option to black and white, rather than color printing which is far more expensive. Another person said, "We're printing out a lot of sheets for meetings. Why don't we print them double-sided them instead of single-sided?" That one small idea cut our paper bills nearly in half.

What else can you do to save? I'd suggest you annually review all your current vendor agreements, especially your employer benefits programs. Owners don't realize that products like group health insurance or group life plans can fluctuate in price from one year to the next. Insurance gets cheaper depending on the size of your company; sometimes if you bundle all of these kinds of programs with one vendor you can save significantly. Reviewing employer benefits is one of the first steps we take when a client asks us to help them find more cash flow, not only to save money but also to potentially increase the programs' value.

Many firms think these kinds of programs are "set it and forget it," but failing to review them can cost real money. We saved one of my clients over $100,000 just by switching from one insurance carrier to a competing one. The kicker was that the original carrier came back to them when they learned they were changing companies and offered them the same savings! The lesson there is that sometimes vendors are willing to negotiate discounts if you let them know you're considering taking your business elsewhere.

An effective tool to use when negotiating with any vendor on any new or renewal agreement is to ask for an additional 10 percent reduction just before signing. Just ask. The worse they can say is "no." My clients and I have saved tens of thousands of dollars doing this.

Another way to encourage your employees to save your company money is to incentivize them financially. If you start offering your people a bonus of 10 percent of the savings they find, you'll be amazed at how creative they get.

Is everyone in your company selling? Of course they are. No matter what kind of company you are, including all of your employees in a sales incentive program is worth doing. Whether it's the receptionist, a senior person on your management staff, or someone in the stock room, let them know that if they bring in a referral that turns into a new client, they'll be rewarded with a percentage of the first year's sale.

USING CASH RESERVES
TO BUY SAVINGS

Do you have significant cash reserves? If so, you might want to consider offering your landlord the year's rent in advance, in exchange for paying only for ten or eleven months rather than the full twelve. This offer may be particularly attractive during economically challenging times, or if there are vacancies in the building and the landlord needs that cash flow now. Sit down with the landlord and see if you can get a discount or renegotiate your lease. It's a good idea to call up your equipment leasing company every so often and see if you can get a better deal, or to compare the lease costs to the costs of a bank loan, which may be lower. I recently wrapped up refinancing a lease arrangement. The company wanted to charge me 10 percent of the fair market value of the equipment to get out of the deal. I called up the bank that used them to complain. As a good customer and referral source to the bank, they had this waived. It saved my company $20,000.

Another place to find cash flow is by refinancing your bank loans for longer-term or interest-only loans. Why? If you understand the principle of compounding and the Tax Savings Savings Effect laid out in earlier chapters, you can see that putting off paying off these loans or stretching them out for as long as possible lets you take advantage of compounding to build your own wealth. Since you don't get a tax deduction for paying principal on a loan, stretching out payments will also decrease your income taxes. In tough economic times, you'll find your bank much more accommodating, either because they're desperate for business, or they've experienced more recent bad loans.

When my business almost went under thirty years ago, one thing I learned was that having cash reserves was extremely important. For one thing, you never again have to depend on a bank. A bank is not your friend, especially in tough times, and having that cash puts you in a great position to bargain with vendors, banks, or insurance companies. If you've been a good client, they'll be eager to serve you especially when they know you have the cash.

As Michael Gerber, author of *The E-Myth*, points out, it's important for every business to scale as much as possible. If you don't have streamlined and efficient processes for handling workflow or customer interactions, you're going to wind up paying for more staff time. In our case as a wealth management company, one of our services is providing financial plans. We've instituted a process for everyone to follow in doing so, which speeds the work and insures that it's high quality and consistent. We know how much time it should take when done according to these guidelines, which makes it easy for us to see who's working efficiently and who is not.

OUTSOURCING SAVES OVERHEAD.

Whenever possible, you should look for ways to outsource services. One of the most obvious examples is payroll: it's much less expensive to pay services like ADP or Paychex a nominal monthly fee to handle payroll for your company than it is to keep people on staff to provide that service. You might also consider leasing or out-sourcing employees. Not only do you save valuable office space by outsourcing, you may also avoid payroll taxes and employee benefits or find them less costly under these arrangements. In situations where you only need extra hands at certain times of the year or for special projects, consider bringing in independent contractors rather than hiring employees or paying overtime.

Another way to conserve cash flow is to pay your employees once a month, rather than twice a month or weekly. This allows you to hang onto your cash for that extra period of time, and means you're reaping the added savings of reducing the number of times your payroll service has to do your payroll from twenty-four to twelve times a year. With that one change in how you do business, you not only preserve cash flow, but your payroll service bills go down.

Also, depending on the size of your payroll, if you're paying employees less frequently, you pay your payroll tax to the government less frequently, too.

HOW ARE YOU PAYING OTHERS—AND HOW ARE YOU GETTING PAID?

Many businesses, especially if they're flush with cash, will get a bit lazy and bill a client expecting to be paid in thirty to ninety days. Yet when they pay their own bills, they'll pay them within fifteen or thirty days. If you're trying to conserve your cash flow, make sure that your customers are paying you on the same schedule as you're paying your vendors. If you're paying your vendors as the bills come in, but your own customers aren't paying you for ninety days, you're effectively financing your customers' businesses for them.

Just ask Rachel Braun Scherl about her experiences doing business with large companies: "Many of them pay us ninety days after a purchase order—and by the way, it sometimes takes ninety days to get a purchase order. In addition, we often pay up-front for project related expenses. We do our very best to get payment for

50 percent of the work up-front. Situations like these make it very difficult for young companies today."[15]

Your vendors may threaten you with a finance charge if you try to change your payment schedule past their stated time limit. This is an opportunity to discuss the terms of your agreement; explain that because of the way your business runs and the schedule on which your customers pay you, you need to pay them on the same schedule on which you're paid, but you don't want to pay that service charge. Alternately, if you have the cash reserves you need to pay them but you're looking for another source of cash flow, suggest that you are willing to pay them ahead of schedule if they're willing to give you a 10 percent or 15 percent discount. Some will agree to these terms, some won't, but it pays to always ask.

Banks like to collect their loan origination and loan closing fees, especially from commercial enterprises, but if you have a lot of cash reserves in your bank, I'd strongly suggest sitting down and renegotiating the fees you're paying, with the aim of getting them eliminated altogether.

As a general rule, always ask for a reduced price in any business relationship. No matter what people present to you as their fixed price, ask for a discount, and you'll be surprised how often you'll get it.

As a general rule, always ask for a reduced price in any business relationship. No matter what people present to you as their fixed price, ask for a discount, and you'll be surprised how often you'll get it. My COO is always surprised at how successful this gambit is: no matter what vendors or service providers we're meeting with, I always ask for a reduced price, and very often get it.

---

15   Rachel Braun Scherl, interview with author.

When I had problems with my own firm, one issue was that I wasn't keeping good track of our receivables and collecting them well. At one point, I had over $500,000 in receivables—right at the point when a recession hit and my company started to get less business from clients. Subsequently, I lost about half of that money because my clients couldn't pay me. This put me in a tight cash flow bind, which I swore never to get into again. And I haven't!

The ideal is not to have anyone owing you money. However, if you do have receivables, make sure you have someone watching them along with you, and that person is someone who is able to deal with people and takes the job of collecting seriously. Whenever I go into a company that's having cash flow issues, one of the first people I sit down with is the person in charge of the billing and collections. I ask that person whether they like asking for money or don't like that about their job. Too often, what I hear is, "I can't stand calling up people and asking for money." If that's the case in your company, you need to move that person out of that job, because they're certainly not going to do it well. But the best approach is to structure your business to eliminate receivables altogether.

If you're not getting paid in a timely way, you're inevitably going to have cash flow crunches. At my firm, we used to send people their bills at the beginning of the month for the prior month, and if they didn't pay within thirty days we'd have to call them. We changed our system to eliminate that: now, when a new client joins us, they pay half of their fees up front and the other half when we have concluded the work, before the work is delivered. Other clients may pay a retainer for our work: if their project is going to be a $100,000 project over six months, we'll ask for a retainer of $15,000 or $20,000. When we send out the bill the following month, they have to pay that to maintain that deposit with us. Should they decide not to pay their bills, we're not out anything.

And are you charging your customers interest on unpaid bills? You should be—most of them will pay it without quibbling. If they do complain, you can tell them, "if you pay the bill now, I'll waive the interest." Use this as a tool to just get paid.

CONSIDER RAISING YOUR PRICES.

While this is often the last thing people think of, raising your prices is a good way to generate more cash flow. Owners feel shy about raising prices for customers. I've told the story elsewhere in this book about the busy consultant who wanted a better lifestyle but still wanted to be able to save for retirement. At the time, he was charging $5,000 a day. We suggested he raise that fee to $10,000 and eventually to $15,000. Initially he balked: "My clients will never agree to it."

We said, "Then don't change your fees for your current clients, but charge everyone who comes to you from now on these higher fees." He was already busy, so he had nothing to lose, and went ahead and doubled his fees to new clients. To his astonishment, they paid! He went back to his current clients and told them he was doubling their fees, and nearly all of them agreed to that. Now he has the lifestyle he wants, more time to enjoy life, and a much higher income.

CONSIDER VALUE BILLING.

Many people who charge a fixed price for hourly services or for a product aren't considering whether the scarcity of what they're offering has value in and of itself, or whether, at times, the need of the client allows them an opportunity to charge more. Those people should weigh the cash flow benefits of value billing.

If you're working on an hourly basis, consider charging instead on a project basis and charging a higher fee. This doesn't just apply to professional services; one of our clients owned a very large printing firm, and much of their work was serving the pharmaceutical companies for whom they print packaging, business cards, etc. Occasionally when these companies put their own promotion folders together they'd discover that something had been left out or was in the wrong order. That left them with the choice of paying one of their own people to go through the twenty thousand folders and insert the missing piece, or sending the whole thing to this printer and hiring his firm to fix it, usually on a rush basis. We suggested that he raise his prices significantly for this, because the value to the customer was so high and the need so urgent. He hired someone at $15 per hour to do the inserts, but charged the client a project fee, so that his company made the equivalent of $200 an hour, easily realizing a profit of $40,000. When you're considering value billing, take into consideration the value of the work to the person paying you, and what resources they have to get it done. Very often you'll find that your customer is happy to pay for the convenience of having the job done for them.

Of course I'm not suggesting that you gouge anyone or do anyone intentional harm. What I am saying is that both you and the other person have a choice. If they want you to stop your production and fit them in, it's only reasonable that they pay you more.

If you're very busy and/or your costs have gone up, take a look at your customer list and apply the Pareto Rule, commonly known as the 80/20 rule. Let's say you have a hundred customers, and you see that 20 percent of your customers or clients produce 80 percent of your income, which is normal. Who's in the bottom 10 percent, and could you replace those customers with others who will pay you more? Raising your prices will often accomplish the same thing. That bottom 10 percent or 20 percent may fall off, but you'll end up having the same amount of top line for fewer customers, less raw materials, and less employment costs, thus making more money.

LOOK FOR OPPORTUNITIES TO ADD SERVICES.

Sometimes the best way to find cash flow is to change direction a bit or pivot. As an example, back when I was having problems keeping my firm afloat, I decided to offer financial planning, a service that didn't require much cost to get off the ground, and which quickly produced added income. Are you keeping track of the changes in your market, and pivoting to offer your customers a product or service they need? It's added value for them, and more business for you.

SAVINGS AND PENSION PLANS CREATE CASH FLOW SAVINGS.

One place few think to look for cash flow savings is establishing a combination 401(k), cash balance pension plan to save tax dollars and take advantage of the Tax Savings Savings Effect. To offer an extreme example, I consulted with a medical practice whose six physician partners were making roughly half a million to $750,000 a year. We showed them how the six of them could shelter about $150,000 each, saving themselves about $450,000 in taxes. Out of that, they put $110,000 into the employees' part of the pension plan, but even so, they were able to shelter and grow $900,000, tax-deferred, so they wound up saving $340,000 in cash flow also.

If you're in a professional association of any kind, find out if they offer group, life, disability, or other kinds of insurance. You're likely to find prices available to you there are significantly lower than other providers.

I realize that all of these ideas require an investment of your time, and that's a commodity we business owners are always short on. But you've got to be willing to work on the business, not just in the business. And if you don't have cash coming in, you may wind up with no business at all.

Chapter 8 Takeaways

- Finding more cash flow requires making well-informed decisions and keeping close track of where the money is going.

- Produce a profit and loss or breakeven statement and a cash flow statement so you can see where you stand on the fifteenth and final days of each month.

- Meet once per month with your management team to review your dashboard, your vital factors, the important indicators or benchmarks for your business.

- Grade your team members annually, and fire C-players immediately, because they're probably costing you serious money.

- Task every member of your management team with coming up with an inventive way to save $250 at each monthly meeting, $50 for other employees, and involve everyone in selling with incentive programs.

- Review all your current vendor agreements, especially your employer benefits programs.

- Look for ways to outsource services and employees.

- Make sure your customers are paying you on the same schedule as you're paying your vendors.

- Raise your prices at every opportunity.

CHAPTER NINE

DEBT: IT'S NOT A FOUR-LETTER WORD

"If you change the way you look at things,
the things you look at change. "
—Wayne Dyer

O r rather, it is, but it's a *good* four-letter word. Most people view any kind of debt as negative, but in fact using debt smarter is a way to grow your business faster, and failing to do so can undermine your growth. Just ask Betty Ng, author, founder and CEO of Inspiring Diversity, LLC, how changing her attitude toward debt has affected her company: "Shedding my innate cultural

Most people view any kind of debt as negative, but in fact using debt smarter is a way to grow your business faster, and failing to do so can undermine your growth.

tendency to carry no debt has enabled me to invest more in my company, for which I expect returns to far exceed what I'm paying in interest, while not having to rely on outside investment."[16]

A current popular founding father, Alexander Hamilton, once commented on debt: "Borrowing money can help a new enterprise or a new nation get started. Debt can build trust, if people borrow money and pay it back on time with interest."

WHY DOES DEBT GET SUCH A BAD RAP?

Our attitudes toward debt are largely a legacy of the twentieth century's Great Depression, which lasted for roughly ten years starting with the market crash of 1929. While most of us weren't alive during the Depression years, we may have parents or grandparents who suffered through it, and we're very familiar with the images of loss and devastation it left—*The Grapes of Wrath*, the grim black and white photographs of men standing in endless breadlines, or of homeless families living in tent encampments. Somehow most of us associate what happened then with debt, but in fact debt had very little to do with it. The real culprit was drought. Farmers then were only a generation removed from the pioneers who'd settled the land, so had little or no debt on their land. But they used to borrow a little every year for their seed money, then pay the bank back after their crops were sold. Until a ten-year cycle of drought turned the Great Plains into a dustbowl, and these farmers lost their farms when they couldn't pay back that seed money or pay their property taxes.

Most people either owned their homes or had short-term loans on them; the thirty-year mortgage was unknown then. Why then did

---

16   Betty Ng, interview with author.

they lose those homes and their businesses? It was because they didn't have sufficient cash reserves. Even though they were likely to own their properties free and clear, they still had to pay real estate taxes. When they couldn't, their properties were seized.

A local bank president I knew when I first started business told me that his father had owned many rental properties during World War II with no mortgages on them, yet lost them all when the war began, because the government instituted rent controls so that rents couldn't go up. Unfortunately, all the associated costs of owning these properties did go up: taxes, maintenance, insurance, etc. His father practically had to give his properties away—again, because he lacked cash reserves. Those who had reserves did fine; those without reserves, even without debt, went under.

But the idea of debt as the villain has stayed with us, and consequently perfectly sound businesses wind up on the rocks because their owners put their cash toward getting out of debt when they should have been holding onto it, thus accelerating their income taxes and leaving them holding an empty bag in the event that they hit a downturn. Even those business owners with an intellectual understanding of the power of compounding and of the impact on wealth of taxes find it difficult to see debt as a positive thing. They're responding to the notion of debt emotionally, rather than rationally. But if they could overcome that knee-jerk reaction, they could begin to see how debt can actually be a powerful partner in building wealth.

USE DEBT TO BUILD WEALTH.

How can you use debt to help build wealth? Say you need $500,000 to buy a piece of equipment, renovate your production facilities, or pay for better employee training—whatever your business needs are.

You might say, "I don't want to have any debt. I have a profit of $50,000 a year. I'll just put that aside, and then when I have the $500,000, I'll buy it." But by the time you've got the money, the equipment and renovation you need could cost more and your better employees may have left. You could invest your savings and maybe with what you earn with your money, the savings would be the same as the price of the equipment ten years from now.

But why not finance it now? Why not expand your top line and your bottom line now? If you incur debt now to expand your business, the profits may also expand and certainly the value of your business will grow too. Maybe you could borrow more than you need, to have cash reserves. You'll have those reserves to keep you safe in case of a downturn, and if you should need to go back to the bank for a line of credit or to refinance your loan, the bank will be more likely to give you what you want if they see you have got reserves to back it up. Banks are not in the business of risk; they're in the business of putting the risk on you. So, a person who has reserves and debt is much less risky to a bank than someone who has no debt but also no reserves.

I worked with a medical corporation whose partners were very eager to pay off the multi-million-dollar debt they'd accrued expanding the business, buying medical equipment and renovating offices. It was a very profitable group, and they didn't see a problem in paying that off in two to four years. But they hadn't considered that in paying off debt, the principal is not a tax deduction; only the interest is. Paying off the millions from the loan principal plus the interest over two to four years really crimped their cash flow. They couldn't understand why they couldn't pay themselves, much less fund their pension. I had to explain that the problem was how they were managing their debt, and that they weren't matching the debt to the life of the asset they'd bought. The machinery would last ten years, yet they were trying to pay it off in three. I suggested they take the debt, go back to the bank and renegotiate it for a ten-year loan. The bank was happy to give it to them.

That way, instead of having to pay accelerated principal, they paid a lot less, thus easing their cash flow problem. By the way, these were smart, highly educated people, but they were less than literate when it came to finance. They knew what a loan was. They knew what taxes were. But they didn't understand compounding or cash flow management.

In another case, I was called in to advise a business that owned a group of retail stores, including the property in which the stores operated. They were in the process of refinancing a $2 million loan on one of the properties. Of course, the bank was pushing them to go for a shorter term so that the loan would be paid off in five or ten years. I told the clients, "No, you want it paid off over thirty, but let's settle for twenty years." Predictably, the bank balked at that.

My clients did, too. They said, "We're in our sixties. We're not going to be around for twenty years."

I said, "You don't have to be. Once you decide to sell the business, you can pay off the loan." We were able to bring the bank around to giving them a longer payout, which significantly decreased the cash flow going out monthly to the bank to pay for the loan. They were able to use that cash instead to invest in a new store and more equipment that made their company more profitable.

If you've balked at taking on debt, or are too eager to pay off debt you've got, it might pay you to consider first how that cash flow you're signing away could help grow your business, and rethink your attitude toward debt.

Chapter 9 Takeaways

- Debt can be good for your business, no matter what you were brought up to believe.

- Smart business owners use debt to leverage improvements to their businesses, earn more and raise selling value.

- Don't be in a hurry to pay off debt, because that can put you in a cash crunch.

- Businesses go under because of lack of cash reserves.

- If you have a short-term loan and the payments are draining your cash, renegotiate for a longer term and lower payments.

CHAPTER TEN

RAISING CAPITAL: FINDING MONEY TO GROW THE BUSINESS AND GROW VALUE

"Nothing will work unless you do."
—Maya Angelou

In the previous chapter I discussed shedding the unreasonable fear of debt and learning to use it to grow shareholder value. Another way to grow value is to grow your business, and if your business is growing, it will need capital to feed that growth—the wealth in cash or investments you need to invest in expanding your venture.

When might you need to make a capital investment? If you own a grocery store and you want to open up another location, you've got to rent a property, which means you have to put down a security deposit. You'll probably need to remodel the new location's interior;

you'll have to order inventory to stock the store, and you'll need to add and train new employees to staff it. All of these expenditures take place ahead the store opening, so you'll need money in advance to pay for all of it. What are your options?

If you can see you've got a likely stream of income you can set aside toward that investment, one option is to wait until you've saved up enough to finance it up front. That could take years. Alternately you can borrow money, or potentially sell shares in or a part of your business to an investor. But if your business is growing, you want to do everything you can to protect your shares, the ownership percent of your business. You don't want to start giving this away. What's your best choice?

If your business is growing, you want to do everything you can to protect your shares, the ownership percent of your business. You don't want to start giving this away.

One entrepreneur I know was faced with this problem; he started a business when he was quite young, but needed capital to get it to the next level. He took on three partners, selling each of them 20 percent in exchange for that needed seed money, and the business really took off. Unfortunately, he and his partners didn't see eye to eye, but they owned 60 percent of his enterprise, so he didn't control it any more. Eventually he solved that problem by buying them out, but had he simply borrowed the money in the first place and paid the lender back, he could have avoided the problems he had now.

Most small businesses are started by entrepreneurs who put their own savings at risk to get started, or borrow against a personal asset like their home, or what's called "bootstrapping." Rusty Shelton, founder and CEO of Shelton Interactive, knows this approach well:

"I bootstrapped each of the businesses I have started and that brings a special kind of cash flow challenge because there isn't a huge backstop in terms of cash (or gas for the engine). As such, I approached growth with a bit more of a measured approach to make sure I didn't get too far over my skis."[17]

Some have opened their businesses using their credit cards, but this isn't the best option, because credit card debt is expensive and you don't get good payment terms, so you have to pay it back very quickly. Yes, it's a way to access money quickly, but it also creates tremendous pressure on you and your business. Some people finance their startups with loans from family members or friends. My advice on this is to be sure it's someone you don't care if you ever see again, because relationships can be fractured when money is lost and you can't pay it back. If your business is already up and running and has some assets, you might consider taking out a loan from your bank.

But when you're building a business and need more capital to expand it, there are other potential sources you may not have considered—like your vendors. If you have a vendor who supplies you with hundreds of thousands of dollars' worth or more of material and/ or supplies, they might be someone to approach for a loan: "I need some capital. Would you float me a loan for five or ten years to help me build a business? I'll be buying more from you." That may offer enough incentive to get them to agree to a loan, if you're a good and reliable customer. The downside of borrowing from vendors is that you might not be able to negotiate better contracts with them if they feel they've already invested in your company, and so don't need to give you a price break. And if you can't pay them back as quickly as you'd agreed, those relationships can be damaged going forward. On

---

17   Rusty Shelton, interview with author.

the other hand, if they see you as a sort of partner, they may be more inclined to be forgiving or to renegotiate terms.

Also, as you grow, your customers or clients can be potential lenders for capital borrowing. If you have a key customer or client, you might be able to offer them a return on an investment in your business in exchange for capital to expand it.

Another option is to do what the big companies do: issue your own debt. You can sell bonds to the general public or to friends, family, vendors and clients once you fill out the proper paperwork. This can be a bit more complex, but I have used this in one of my businesses.

BORROW OR SELL SHARES?

What are the advantages of borrowing versus selling shares in your company? Especially if you're a small company, although the interest rate you pay may be high, there are some advantages to consider about borrowing. Instead of having a co-owner that's going to have input into how you run your business, you can shape the company as you wish. You don't have to answer to your lenders as you would to other owners or shareholders. You're free to run the company and take whatever actions you want.

Another nice thing about borrowing is you can always borrow more. You pay off the current loan when you wish to, or if you want to borrow more from a bank or other people, you can if you meet the lender's loan requirements. You can grow the company and not have to dilute the value of the shares. But if you sell 25 percent of your company, you only own 75 percent of the value, versus 100 percent of the value. If you've borrowed the money, you always will own 100 percent of the value.

Finally, you can pay it off whenever you want. If you have the spare cash, you can pay off the debt or, if you find another lender that is cheaper, you can refinance those loans and pay less interest. If you're borrowing from family and friends, it matters less or not at all whether your business is rated A, B, or C, or what your personal credit report looks like.

WHAT ARE THE DISADVANTAGES TO BORROWING?

Now you'll have to pay an interest payment, which means you'll have to add that figure into your outgoing cash flow. The borrowers may want personal guarantees, whether it's your own bond or note, depending on the size of your business. Certainly, if you're borrowing from a bank, they will normally ask for personal guarantees, and that means that if the corporation or company can't pay, you're on the hook.

You may have to disclose personal or family financial information you don't wish to share, and to answer questions about earnings, what your core business is, and what you intend to do with the money. The bank is going to want all your personal data, and they're going to run credit reports on you.

Investors may not like the fact you have debt. If you reach a point at which you've grown in size, and now you want to go public and/or to sell part of the company, your potential investors may demand that you pay off that debt, so it may affect your value. And if you choose to sell the business outright, your buyer may demand that you pay off your debt first or at closing.

There are costs to consider to in putting up your own bond issue. As I said earlier, I did this once in a business I owned. If you choose to issue a bond and your company is large enough, you may have to file with the Securities and Exchange Commission, because a bond, particularly a loan instrument like this, is considered a security. That can add cost, and as regulators, they can demand more information from you. There are ways to get around this—if your offering is small enough, you file a set of forms that shows the SEC that your offering is too small to fall under their scrutiny. Filling out and filing those forms will require a professional's help, and that's another expense to consider.

SELLING EQUITY

So instead of borrowing, what's another alternative? You could sell equity, a part of your company. But others will now own a piece of your company, and you're chipping away at your personal control of your enterprise. The general rule here is that it's better than borrowing if the company's not growing much. If your company is growing and the value of the company is growing faster than what you're paying for the interest on the debt, you're better off borrowing. But you want to keep control.

Let's say your business has flattened out, and you're not seeing much chance for growth going forward. You may wish at that point to sell part of your company and diversify your holdings, so instead of having all your worth tied up in your company, you now have some of your money out in other investments to decrease your own risk. That might be a cheaper way to get capital than to borrow it.

What are the advantages of selling stock in the company? With bonds, you have interest due immediately, but if someone's just buying a share of the company, there's no interest payment due, so no cash issue. And as long as you still control 51 percent of the voting shares, you still control the company. If you fall below that you don't control it anymore, and you're at risk of being replaced by other shareholders.

That said, there are smart ways of selling even a majority of shares in your company while still keeping control. You can control it by having different classes of stock: A shares versus B, voting and nonvoting. You might actually own only 1 or 2 or 10 percent of your company, but you retain all the voting shares. This is one way the founders of big tech firms hold onto control of the companies they started.

You can also sell equity or ownership to your own employees, and at a discount. This provides a great incentive to them to help grow the company. Again, if you're selling equity to friends, family, and other business people, you don't have to worry about your credit rating. If you're going to sell bonds or go to a bank, they're most likely going to check your credit, but with selling shares they normally won't.

At times, borrowing just isn't an option. When you're just starting up and need to raise capital, most people will tell you, "The shares are probably worthless, but I'd agree to lend you money if you had collateral or could pay me interest." If you're just starting out, this is a great way to raise money since you may not be able to do it based on your company's history at that point. Now, if you're selling shares initially, you may be able to borrow in the future as the company's value grows. Once you're able to borrow, you don't have to keep on selling shares if you want to raise capital.

Another potential upside is that since you now have to report to shareholders or other owners, it may actually push you to focus more than you do on profitability and making better decisions in your business. Often, business owners that own 100 percent can get a little lazy with their money; the attitude is, "If I don't make the sales goals, I'm not going to fire myself." But if you have outside owners now and they want to know, "Why are you lagging behind your competitors? Why aren't you making more profit?" you'll have to become a better CEO. When I had other shareholders, I know that their inquiries made me a better CEO.

WHAT ARE THE DISADVANTAGES OF SELLING SHARES?

You'll have to be willing to answer to others regarding your decisions and actions. You'll be expected to perform. If you laid out a business plan to your shareholders when you were selling them shares, you have to show them that you're actually following it. You may not be able to do everything you want. Some outside groups, even if they own only 25 percent, may place restrictions on you so that you can't sell the company, or do this, that, or the other.

Again, you may have to disclose information that might get out to others or to competitors. If you have people that are buying into you, now you're disclosing to them as an owner. Those same people may be at a cocktail party and tell other people information you'd rather wasn't public knowledge.

You may have to file as a different entity. If you were organized as a partnership or an LLC, your corporate structure might have to change to keep you in compliance with the law regarding how you're selling or holding your shares. You may have to have a dividend that you pay out, and a dividend is not a deduction for a corporation. If you have to share profits, you'll be giving out some percentage of them, so you'll no longer be getting 100 percent. And again, just as if you had issued your own bonds, if you're large enough you may have to file with or answer to the SEC.

You may decide you'd rather rely on a bank (eventually, as your company grows, you're almost certainly going to need to borrow from a bank), but as I've said before it's important to remember that banks are not your friends. They want to loan you money when you don't need it and you can absolutely prove you don't need it. But when times aren't so good, they get nervous and want their money back. Remember, banks do not take risks. When you start a business, you're the risk taker. When you issue bonds, you're the risk taker. But banks aren't risk takers. They want to be 100 percent protected if you can't pay. They normally like any borrowing to be short-term, and it's very rare that they offer anything other than a line of credit, which you have to renew annually. They may be willing to fund a loan for computers, furniture, or fixtures for your business, but normally just for three to five years. If you're buying real estate they may give you longer payback terms, but it's still going to be less time than you'd get if you were taking out a personal mortgage loan for a house. Another consideration in borrowing from banks is that they generally have a clause in their lending contract stating that if your business is doing badly, if you're in financial difficulties, or if you pass away, they can call the note and demand payment.

That happened to a late friend of mine, Steve Scebelo, a business owner with commercial properties. He'd been paying on time and the property had a lot of equity in it. But he passed away, and there was a common clause in his lending contract that said if he died, he'd effectively defaulted on the note, and they could demand full payment immediately. This was a sizable note, too—about $750,000 on a property worth more than twice that. I got involved and worked with the bank to extend the note for a period of time so that his heirs could sell the property. But you may not be in a position to sell a property. Or a recession might hit, and your business might suffer accordingly.

Again, with bank borrowing, these loans are normally short-term, so it may be a problem if you're looking for long-term lending. Lastly, they want personal guarantees. If your business is small, even up to $10 million, $20 million or more, depending on the situation they're likely to demand that the primary owner or the owners personally guarantee the loans.

Banks will give you short-term loans or lines of credit for cash flow purposes. Also, if you have a company and the company borrows, it shows up on the company's credit report, but it normally doesn't show up on yours.

WHEN IT COMES TO DEBT, BE CREATIVE.

Look at ways to combine different sources of capital to get the money you need: perhaps selling part of your company, then floating bonds, or getting bank financing. Like I said previously, I did this.

Back around 2010, when banks were not lending, I decided to refinance $1 million in debt my company had for various loans for equipment and renovation, because I realized that some of the loans were short term and at high interest, and by refinancing I could save significant cash flow. At that point I was planning to open another office, and anticipated the expenses involved with that too, so I really needed about $2 million to pay off the debt and have that extra million to fund the expansion. I realized I couldn't get the bank to do it. How could I raise that money?

As I was ruminating about this, I happened to pick up former Secretary of the Treasury Henry Paulson's book, *Inside the Race to Stop the Collapse of the Global Financial System.* Paulson was at one time a co-chair at Goldman Sachs, and was discussing how companies financed themselves through their own debt structures. My company was comparatively small, but why couldn't we do this? That gave me the inspiration to float our own bonds.

I called an attorney who specialized in rules for the Securities and Exchange Commission, got a presentation on how to put it together, and we made an offering of $2.5 million. We were able to do that without ever having to depend on a bank, without worrying about a credit rating, or having to worry about the bank calling the notes on us.

We did have to pay a high interest rate. The rates at that time if you went to a bank were 5 percent, maybe 6 percent. But hey, who cared about rates when you couldn't get a loan? We had to pay 8 percent, but it was a bargain! By consolidating debt and getting better terms, we saved over $75,000 per year. We structured it so it was a ten-year note and no principle had to be paid on the note, just interest twice a year. Even though I had to borrow at 8 percent, I didn't have to go through filings with the bank every year or the expenses associated with that, and I was able to get my money and expand the company. I had control of my company, and no bank looking over my shoulder.

Another way to borrow money is to go to a private equity group. These are companies that have money to lend other companies. They buy into your company, perhaps 25 percent or 40 percent, and they expect to earn money along the way and when you sell the company. I wanted to avoid this. They're going to have either options or another way to get part of the increase in the value of your firm in the time they are invested in it.

HOW WOULD YOU LOOK TO AN INVESTOR?

No matter how you're going to raise capital, whether it's through selling part of the company or borrowing, you're eventually going to have to present a picture of your business finances to your potential lender so that they're confident enough in your finances to loan you money. But too often business owners inadvertently take actions in their businesses that make them look bad to lenders, undercutting their chances of getting the loan they need.

One business owner I worked with has grown his company sales to $5 million. He was expanding rapidly, and the future looks really bright for him, but he was taking all of his profits and plowing them back in the business, so his bottom line appeared to be very small, even though he actually was doing very well.

I asked him, "What does a company in your industry normally get as a profit margin?"

He told me, "Somewhere between 15 percent to 20 percent." But his profit margin was much smaller because he was investing in the company—equipment, software, training—and he was writing it all off. Even though he was building potential and value, if you read his financial statements you'd have to wonder why he wasn't making anything, and would probably write him off as a risky investment.

I suggested to him that he should have two sets of books. Large corporations have many sets of books based on what they're trying to present. This does not mean they're trying to hide anything; it's all very transparent. But this client needed what is called a tax set of books, as well as a set of "real" books for the company following established accounting rules.

How does this work? Let's say for that year he could have shown a profit of $750,000, but he used the $750,000 to buy more equipment, set up another office, or do training, etc. This got him tax breaks and saved valuable cash flow, but for his financial books what he wants to do is record that the $750,000 was actually going to be written off over five or ten years, so that on the books he'd show a profit, but on his tax return books he can show there's no profit. That's the smarter way to do it, because he'd look better to banks and the people who make decisions about loans.

It all comes down to knowing what readers of your financial statements want to see, and what red flags they're looking for. Rule one is to always be honest, of course. But different accounting rules apply to how you report earnings depending on what you're required to show to whom.

MAKE SURE YOUR FINANCIAL HOUSE IS IN ORDER.

In assessing a business for loans or investments, your potential investor will expect to see financial statements. It's just like selling your house: when you're preparing to sell your house, you make it look as good as you can. You clear out the clutter, and put a fresh coat of paint on it. It's the same thing with financial statements. Make sure your house is in order, and that everything looks clean and transparent. That's what investors and lenders are looking for. Remember, the question is always going to be, "What's in it for me or my financial institution?" If you can show them that their money isn't at risk and that they'll make money lending to or investing in you, you're much more likely to get the capital you need.

Chapter 10 Takeaways

- At some point your business may need capital, whether for expansion, new equipment, or training.

- Don't use your credit cards for capital unless you absolutely have to.

- One way to raise capital is to sell shares, but you're also selling a piece of your ownership, and may lose control of your own enterprise.

- Financing your business with loans from family or friends can have negative consequences if the business runs into trouble and they lose their investments.

- You can try to borrow from your vendors, who know you as a good and reliable customer and have a vested interest in your growth. Customers or clients can also be approached for a loan.

- You can choose to issue your own debt but must weigh the costs of filing with the SEC, and deal with other complexities.

- Get creative! Look at ways to combine different sources of capital to get the money you need, perhaps selling part of your company, then floating bonds or getting bank financing.

CHAPTER ELEVEN

BE A SAVVY INVESTOR—IN
YOUR OWN BUSINESS

"The way to get started is to quit talking and begin doing."
—Walt Disney

What's your business's greatest asset? Is it your clients, your inventory, your property? Could it be a trademark or proprietary processes you own? What should you be focusing on for greater sales and profitability?

Over the years I've been in business, I've realized my company's most valuable asset is my people, and I think most business owners would agree with me. I've talked at length on topics like the CFO mind-set, the business Wealth Building Formula®, and on finding capital to grow your business, and all of those things are critical to success. But nothing has a greater impact on your bottom line than the excellence of your team. To find the right people, train them, and get them on board, while syncing them with your vision and mission, is an expensive and time-consuming process. But if you don't have great people interacting with your customers, you won't have those customers for long, so it's the most important investment you can make.

What's the best investment you can make in your team? I'd suggest it's better communication. If you're not conveying your vision for your company going forward to the people tasked with realizing that vision, it's like a rudderless ship drifting wherever the currents take it. But a team that understands and is invested in your vision can pull together to get you where you want to go. Companies like Johnson & Johnson, Volvo, and other leaders in their fields do a great job of giving their people grasp of the mission and the vision of the company, and how they fit into it.

A big piece of good communication is letting your team members know where they stand. Are they contributing up to the level you expect, or are they lagging? I talked in an earlier chapter about grading team members, especially in reviews, so that they have a chance to upgrade their performance if it's not up to a high standard. It's not fair to expect them to read your mind, nor can they reasonably expect you to carry them if they're not doing the job in the way you need them to. Being clear with team members about where they stand is a way to help them self-correct, and gives them the opportunity to do so. Remember, an "A" or a "B" team member makes you money, but a "C" employee is costing you money, and carrying substandard employees is a luxury you can't afford.

How can you avoid saddling yourself with the kinds of employees who will lose you money? Hire slowly and fire quickly. You want to take your time in hiring, but if you discover after you've hired that the person's a bad fit for the job or your company, it's best for all concerned if they're let go as expeditiously as possible. If you were fielding a football team, and accidently drafted a basketball player, you'd let him go immediately. How is he going to help get the football down the field? Even if he was a great basketball player, your team isn't the place for him. Get him off the team quickly, because until you do, the team will be less effective than it could be.

MAKE MEETINGS MORE PRODUCTIVE.

Your investment in great communication should include regular staff meetings and management meetings. Division leaders should be holding regular meetings with their staff also. But don't let these turn into free-for-alls; make sure that whoever's running the meeting has an agenda, and that everyone's clear and focused on the issues to be discussed. In our firm, staff members run staff meetings, not the management. We encourage openness and honesty: people should feel free and secure enough to bring up whatever issues concern them. I think a lot of managers and owners reading this would cringe at the idea of someone at a staff meeting saying, "We don't think we're paid enough," but I strongly suggest you look for and encourage those moments, because they give you an opportunity as an owner or part of the management team to address that problem head on.

And when a staff person does come into a meeting with a volatile topic for discussion and takes the risk of bringing it up not only in front of management but the whole staff, you want to congratulate them. You want to honor them. You want to make sure they're acknowledged for that, because that encourages others to be similarly open and communicative. And most importantly, you want to answer those questions!

I remember an incident at my own company when Charlene Maruska, a senior administrator, confronted me—the CEO—in my office, for having been unduly brusque to her. I could see she was on the verge of tears as she took me to task, and that it took real courage for her to call me out on my behavior—and she was right.

There were two ways I could have handled this: by dismissing her with a half-baked apology, or by thanking her for her candor, and apologizing from the heart. I chose the second option, telling her, "I really appreciate the fact that you would take the risk to come and speak to me and be so honest." I asked her in fact to bring it up at the next staff meeting. Why? So that I'd have the chance to let our people know that as CEO of the company I encourage that type of open communications within our company.

Another reason to have regular meetings is to rally the troops, because it's important to remind your people about your mission and vision and their place in it. Don't just "set it and forget it." Your team has to be reminded of why the company exists. At staff meetings and other meetings we have in the company, we spend part of our meetings on role-playing, and everyone participates, from the CEO to the receptionist. One person takes on the role of a client, another takes on the role of a team member who's tasked with answering questions like, "Who is Mercer Advisors? Why should I come to you?" There are standard answers to questions like that, and it's good to give people a chance to repeat them and remind people of who we are and what we do.

GET CLEAR ON YOUR COMPANY CULTURE.

According to a 2015 Harvard Business Review article "How Company Culture Shapes Employee Motivation," business owners generally agree that a strong company culture is critical to success, but that it "... tends to feel like some magic force that few know how to control." [18] Like anything else in business, it takes dedication and constant work to grow and protect a culture.

Staff meetings also give you a chance to talk about your company culture. In our company, we don't allow gossip; you cannot walk into another person's office and say something about someone else that you wouldn't say to his or her face. By making sure that everyone understands that's a core value, we're also underscoring the fact that the rule is there to protect everyone—for their benefit—and our team appreciates that.

Make part of your culture showing appreciation for team members. That's important whether it's coming from you as the head or from one team member to another. Over twenty years ago we adopted a practice I read about in a book called *Zapp! The Lightning of Empowerment* by William Byham and Jeff Cox, which advocates giving team members "zapps." At the end of a team meeting, our people can choose to give each other zapps, which are acknowledgments to staff or to management of things that they did during the last week that were really in alignment with the mission of the company, or made other team members feel positive about their actions.

A zapp can be something like, "Mary went out of her way to send Mrs. Jones the information she requested so quickly. She was a

---

18   Lindsay McGregor, and Neel Doshi. "How Company Culture Shapes Employee Motivation." *Harvard Business Review*, November 25, 2015, https://hbr. org/2015/11/how-company-culture-shapes-employee-motivation.

great example of client service," or, "Rick stayed hours past closing to make sure he could meet Mr. Smith and take care of his problem. A great example of our mission." Acknowledging individual team members is an uplifting and positive way to end a meeting.

LET PEOPLE KNOW WHERE THEY STAND.

I mentioned performance reviews, but investing the time it takes to give team members individual feedback shouldn't be a once-a-year event. While you may give a formal annual review, nobody should ever be surprised by what their review will say. And if you've had clear communication throughout the year, they won't be. Everyone should know where they stand when that annual review comes around, which gives you a chance to talk about the next year's goals for them and the company.

We use scorecards (another idea I adopted from *Who*) to help increase everyone's clarity around both shared and individual goals, and through these, to better support the goals of the company. Everyone in the company has a scorecard, which lists what the individual's goals should be, and how they support the company's goals. These are reviewed during the year to see whether or not they've moved closer to accomplishing those goals. Even our firm as a whole has its own scorecard, which management reviews at least monthly and   helps us all see how the company is achieving its goals during the year and if we have to make adjustments, pivot, or do something else to move closer to our goals.

With new team members, performance reviews should be done every three months for the first year, along with extensive onboarding when they first join your enterprise so there's clarity about what's expected of them. Our onboarding process takes three days: the new hire meets the team, learns how to open the office, how the computer systems work, and is introduced to the company's mission and vision. The more that know people coming in, the faster they can adapt and get up to speed. It also gives them a sense of belonging and team sooner.

It's important as a leader that you set an example of interpersonal honesty: never patronize people by being less than forthright when it comes to your observations and their performance.

It's important as a leader that you set an example of interpersonal honesty: never patronize people by being less than forthright when it comes to your observations and their performance. If you see problems between team members, step in and address them. Otherwise you're creating a situation in which issues can fester unresolved and take peoples' attention away from their work.

LEARNING NEVER STOPS.

Ongoing learning and development are other important investments you need to make in your team. Everyone needs to be in constant development within your industry and in their special niche. All of our management goes through the MAP Management System™ leadership program, for instance. This gives the tools to management to focus on goals.

You also want to make sure that your people belong to the appropriate professional or local community organizations, because they learn through networking and learning about other professionals' best practices.

Invest in bringing in consultants or in-house coaches to work with your team, your managers, and you. We started using coaches almost thirty years ago to help with team building, but they're also great resources to help communication in our enterprise. People are not normally built as communication machines; our thoughts are generally filtered if we express them at all. A coach can help people break through those social restraints and express themselves more honestly. We've worked with Dr. David Zelman, the founder of Transitions Institute in Dallas, Texas, for almost twenty years. He's trained our people in communicating with peers and clients, handling tough issues, and even self-awareness, and his help has been invaluable. We would not be the firm we are today without his help and the help of many other consultants.

GET YOUR BUSINESS A MENTOR.

Invest time in finding connections with a mentor or mentors. Most companies that get off to a successful start and continue that way have a mentor, someone that will help guide them. Even if you've been in business for a while, it's still a good practice, because you can always learn from someone more experienced or expert than you. Look for someone who's been more successful than you, or has a bigger company, better processes, or who is more innovative than you have been. Ideally, you want to have at least one or two mentors that you connect with once a month, whether that's over lunch or via telephone. Ask them to recommend you to others whose knowledge or experience you might benefit from. I have never had a contact that I've asked, "Whom should I be speaking to?" who hasn't come up with one or two names for me.

Having trouble finding some mentors? You might consider joining a local chapter of an organization like Vistage® CEO Network or Entrepreneur's Organization (EO). You may find business owners and executives that will share like problems and solutions. Jamie McIntyre has made good use of his Vistage group: "Every month, each of these CEOs discussed their business issues (cash flow and otherwise) and they became strong collaborative mentors regardless of their industry. All of these relationships continue to be invaluable."[19]

Having an advisory board is another kind of mentorship worth investing in, because as you grow as a company, it's tremendously helpful to have a group to bounce new ideas off of or weigh in on your decisions. You can learn a lot by listening to them discuss the merit or lack of merit to ideas and innovations you want to introduce. This is not the same thing as a board of directors, but a more informal yet still independent group.

Let's say you want to gather together four or five people that are in your industry to form your board of advisors. They could be outside of it, but they've either all run, or are the heads of successful companies. Once you've gotten signed non-compete and confidentiality agreements from them, you let them look at everything you're doing. You give them permission to tear you apart. You give them permission to ask anything they want, with the goal of making yours a better company. You want their unvarnished opinions on what they're seeing. Even if this is just two or three people convening every quarter, you will find that it's one of the greatest investments a business can make in itself. It was my greatest investment!

A word of caution: Never invite a client to be on your board. You're almost certain to feel some degree of constraint, and may not be as open about issues or problems your company has in front of

---

19   Jamie McIntyre, interview with author.

a client. Also, it's very hard to fire a client in a case where they've outlived their usefulness as a board member, aren't really active participants, or just aren't showing up for meetings. The same goes for major vendors: you don't want them on your board. You're going to be talking about processes and other confidential things, and even though you've got their signed agreements, you don't want to risk those things getting out to the general public, and you certainly don't want the vendor knowing what the weak spots in your company are.

You do want some members who are either successful in your industry, or outside of but familiar with the industry. You want people that have dealt with the same issues that you have now—founders or CEOs—and who can talk about how they solved them.

TO PAY OR NOT TO PAY?

Should you pay your advisory board members? Some do, because their time is valuable. In our case, our board meets quarterly, and we treat them to a nice dinner, but we don't pay them. We've had some people turn down our invitation to join the board because it's not paid, and large, successful, and serious-minded people are fine with it, because most successful people want to contribute to others or to share what they've learned along the way. I would much prefer to have someone who simply wants to contribute versus someone who's just there for the paycheck. This is personal preference and up to you to decide.

That said, these are busy people and you don't want to waste their time. Make sure you have agendas, that you cover important topics, and that you're asking them for advice and guidance, not just lecturing them on what the company's done in the last quarter. Whenever we add a new board member, I read them the ground rules: what they're responsible for and what we're responsible for. They're given complete permission to say anything, and shouldn't feel as if they have to hold anything back. Most of all don't be defensive. Listen to what they have to say and thank them for their input, whether you agree with it or not.

Whether or not you're paying them, an advisory board requires an investment of your time and money. You're paying for these people to travel to you, sometimes to stay overnight, and at minimum providing a dinner. Your time as a participant and that of other key managers who attend is also a cost, so it behooves you to get as much as you can in terms of value from the meetings. Make sure that your board members are also getting value from the experience. Our board members make valuable contacts with each other that often lead to business transactions, and we usually refer business to them whenever we can. Ideally everyone involved gains value from this experience.

If you want to be someone who works on your business as well as in your business, don't neglect these kinds of investments in communication, growth, and development. Your team is your greatest asset, because your business rises or falls based on their efforts and cohesion. No matter how much investment you make in things like technology, infrastructure, or expansion, failure to invest significantly and on an ongoing basis in your team will get in the way of your company's growth.

Chapter 11 Takeaways

- Your most valuable business asset is your team members.

- The best investment you can make in enabling your team is great communication. Make sure your team members feel safe and empowered to share their views, even if they're critical of you.

- A big piece of good communication is letting your team members know where they stand. Don't neglect giving praise, often and publicly.

- Every business owner needs mentors: trusted, savvy, and experienced people who can offer advice. Don't be afraid to ask someone more successful than you are for their insights.

- Invest in coaching for you, your management team, and staff.

- Learning should be a continuing process, and ongoing training is a great way to help your team to grow and your business to prosper.

- Consider putting together an advisory board to help you make important decisions.

CHAPTER TWELVE

SUCCESSION AND CONTINGENCY PLANNING: PROTECTING THOSE WHO COUNT ON YOU

"Those who are victorious plan effectively and change decisively."
—Sun Tzu

I t's the topic nobody really wants to consider: What happens to your business if a key player—maybe even you—suffers sudden disability or death? What can you do to protect your hard-won assets? Alternately, when it's time to make the choice to retire or sell your enterprise, what can you do to make the process easier and less fraught with potential pitfalls when that time comes?

If this subject makes you uncomfortable, you're not alone. One online provider of legal resources, Rocket Lawyer, claims that approximately 72 percent of entrepreneurs they surveyed did not have a succession plan in place for their business. Whether it's because they're too busy, they assume they don't need it, or they think they're going to live forever, failure to plan properly for your exit from the business can create big problems down the line for you, your potential buyers, or your heirs.

But it's your responsibility as a CEO or owner to look ahead, even if your exit most likely won't take place for many years, and to consider how your business going to run without you. For one thing, having a succession plan allows you to retire if you want to, while assuring a smooth transition of the business to the new management, to your partners, or to other people that you've grown within the company. It also compels you as the leader of your team to surround yourself with A-players to assure that smooth transition. Whereas if you're just assuming you'll be at the wheel forever, which gives you an excuse to shrug off having a second-rate team.

> *It's your responsibility as a CEO or owner to look ahead, even if your exit most likely won't take place for many years, and to consider how your business going to run without you.*

Having a great management team has the additional benefit of increasing the value of your business to potential buyers or investors. It's also a big plus when negotiating with vendors or banks, because they prefer doing business with well-managed companies, and are likely to offer you more advantageous terms. Given that your business is almost certainly your most valuable asset, not having a succession plan in hand seems foolhardy to me, especially since that's going to have a tremendous impact on your wealth or the wealth of your loved ones and their heirs.

A SOLID SUCCESSION PLAN IS SMART RISK MANAGEMENT.

The stronger your succession plan, the less risk you have for yourself, your loved ones, your team, and your clients or customers. Even if you're not all that concerned with it personally, you should think of how failure to plan for the future could impact those who depend on you. And if you're getting closer to retirement age, believe me: your clients have noticed and are probably wondering what the next step is. I've had clients ask me as I've gotten older, "Al, we love you, but what's going to happen if you're not around?" You can actually harm your business if you don't plan, because the client wonders what the next step is going to be and who's going to take care of them, so they may start to look elsewhere as a precaution.

There was a firm that my company dealt with for years; they supplied great service, and the owner was terrific, but he was in his mid-seventies with no clear number two in sight. I remember sitting down with him saying, "Look, we do a lot of business with you and we'd like to know what the succession plan is, who's taking over, or else we may have to start looking for another supplier somewhere down the road."

He assured us he was taking care of it, but years passed and all of a sudden, he was pushing eighty, yet still had no succession plan. Faced with that uncertainty, we felt it was prudent to find ourselves another supplier. He was still running the firm very well, but looking ahead we could see there was likely to be chaos when he either passed away or retired, because he was so central to his company's operation and success. Assuaging your customers' concerns about your successor is a way to keep their confidence in your firm's stability over the long run and keep them as customers in the meanwhile.

Many owners put off making a succession plan, because they just can't imagine abandoning their "baby." Having poured so much of their lives into building a business, exiting it seems like a sort of death, and a harbinger of mortality. Add to that the fact that most business owners are very much engaged in the day to day running of their enterprise and it's clear why succession planning gets shoved to the back burner too much of the time.

HAVE A CONTINGENCY PLAN.

More important than a succession plan is having a contingency plan. You should focus on this plan first. Many people confuse these, but they're different, so let's define our terms.

A *succession plan* lays out the planning for the eventual smooth transition of the company from one generation to the next, or from one owner or set of owners or management team to another. You've got time to do that, and to put the people to whom you'll pass the reins in place and prepare them for their roles.

But suppose it's not smooth. Suppose that either the majority owner or the head of the company or a key player becomes ill, is involved in an accident, or dies suddenly. That could cast management into chaos, and even put the company out of business. An owner, especially one whose businesses employ fewer than five hundred employees—is normally a key person: the CEO, a top salesperson on whose expertise the business depends. They're usually also the face of the business, the person most familiar to the customers or clients. What happens immediately, if that person is suddenly unable to continue in his or her role? This is when having a contingency plan in place is like throwing your company a lifeline.

WHAT GOES INTO A CONTINGENCY PLAN?

As the owner, it's important that you leave instructions behind that detail your goals and wishes for the future of the business. This document needs to be in the hands of someone or a group of people you trust, either inside the company or with an appointed outside advisor, and should include important business information, such as the names of trusted advisors, accountants, attorneys, and financial advisors, so that the proper people can be contacted.

It should detail other key confidential information, any kind of agreements, and where key documents are stored. Is there a safe deposit box? Is there a will, insurance policies, or bank accounts? What passwords are needed to access these? Where are liquid assets located? Obviously, as the key person in your enterprise, you should be talking to your management team and getting them involved, making sure this information is disseminated before the need for it arises, but most of the time, owners fail to do this.

Your contingency plan should also name your successor, whether permanent or temporary, who can step up to operate the company, and vote or control your owner shares. Should the company be sold, or do you wish it to continue to operate? Who is empowered to make that decision?

I was sitting down with a business owner whose company had sales in excess of $25 million. He was working on a succession plan but had no contingency plan. He did have one very long and highly detailed letter to his spouse explaining to her how to run the company, how to sell it, how to get the best officers, etc. Now, his wife had no business experience at all, had never had anything to do with his company, and had no negotiating experience. He asked me if I thought this detailed letter was sufficient as a contingency plan.

I had to tell him, "She's not going to be able to handle this. For one thing, if something happens to you, keep in mind that she and your whole family will be deep in grief and in no condition to handle the business's day-to-day affairs. There will be a period where she'll have to deal with your personal affairs, apart from the business. And how in the world is your wife supposed to run the company, with no experience and only this letter to guide her? The company will be plunged into chaos, because you've got no real contingency plan. The good people on your team may immediately going to be looking for work elsewhere seeing there is no future for the company, so you'll be losing key people, key assets, from the start."

How is a good contingency plan assembled? Here's how one sixty-two-year-old founder handled it. He decided he needed a succession plan, as he was looking to transition out of his business over the next five or ten years, and wanted a smooth transition. He asked his board of advisors for help in drafting it, but they convinced him that what he needed first was a contingency plan, because he already had a capable and informed team in place that could provide a smooth succession.

This CEO held the majority of shares of the company, some of which were held in trusts, and some by him personally. It took two years to put a solid contingency plan together that answered questions like who would run the company.

In the plan, three members of the current board of advisors would step up to become outside members of a board of directors along with the current chief operating officer (COO) and current executive vice president of the company. Three outside directors would be tasked with controlling the shares of the founder and the trust. Why? He wanted the most experienced people—outsiders who were the CEOs of other successful companies—to control the future of his company. The two other minority shareholders, the COO and executive vice president, were also on the board, but they would not be able to control the majority of the shares.

The COO, who was then second in command of the company, would be made temporary CEO and the board would decide to keep him on long-term or not. The board would also decide if the company was sold or stayed in operation. Minority shareholders would be given first option to buy.

The founder and majority owner was able to tell these people ahead of time what the vision and purpose of the company and what his wishes were, that his clients and the team would be taken care of as well as they possibly could be, and that he left it to the outside members of his board of directors to decide whether the company should be sold or not. Thus, when clients and others began to ask him what the plan was if something should happen to him, he was able to give them a clear and reassuring answer. He explained it to his staff too, because he wanted them to be reassured the enterprise wouldn't plunge into chaos if he passed away.

WHAT HAPPENS WHEN YOU FAIL TO PLAN?

I talked earlier in the book about Steve Scebelo, a very close friend of mine since college. He was a former business partner who had established a successful CPA tax practice twenty years ago. After many years of successfully fighting cancer, he took a rapid and unexpected turn for the worse and suddenly passed away. This was a shock and heartbreak for all who cared about him, but a disaster too for those who'd depended on him—his clients, his staff, his family—because he had failed to plan. He died without a contingency plan.

We had promised each other over twenty years before that in the event anything happened to either of us, the other would be there for his family. We didn't put it in writing. We didn't have to; we were that close. But about six months before his death, I was having dinner with him and his family and it was clear he was not well. So, I got him alone, and being a close friend, he allowed me to say, "You do not look good. It is clear your family is worried. I hope you get back to full health, but I want to make sure you've taken care of everything necessary if you don't. Is everything in order—your will, your papers, your insurance?"

He assured me, "Yes, everything is in order, but I'm going to beat this." He had done it so many times, so you had to believe he would again. This time, he didn't.

Over the next few months, we stayed in frequent contact. I had found out from his wife he was doing badly. Seeing him just a week before his death he told me he'd been given three months to live. As extremely close and caring friends must do, I had a tough conversation with him. Though we were the best of friends, I asked his permission to speak to him, as I'd hope he'd speak to me under similar circumstances, and he agreed.

I told him bluntly, "You may not have three months, and you don't know what those three months will bring. You may not be ambulatory. You may be in the hospital, or even comatose." He'd previously asked me to review his important papers—his wills, trusts, and other critical documents—and I told him I wanted to get started on those.

He said, "Look, I was just told a few days ago I have three months to live. I'm still trying to absorb that. Can we do this in a few days?"

I knew I couldn't push him any more in this meeting so I said, "Okay."

It was a mistake. I went home and within two days, his wife called me up to tell me he was in the hospital. I went to see him, but he could barely talk. The doctor told us he probably had a day or two. I tried to ask Steve where those papers were, but he was too far-gone to answer accurately.

Nobody knew where these critical documents were; I went through his office for days, practically tearing it apart trying to find them. His attorney had a copy of the will, but nobody knew where the original was, not even his wife. She had no picture of what their finances looked like; she had no clue about the running of his practice. He'd had some preliminary talks with staff about taking over but he'd never put anything in writing.

We got a copy of the will from one of the attorneys, but we eventually had to go to court and spend time and money to get his wife declared the executrix because he didn't have an original. He had commercial property and other investments, and once the banks found out he had died, they started to foreclose on the properties. We eventually got them to give us time, but it took months to negotiate with the bank, because they were going to foreclose on valuable property and were worried about the loans against them.

He had vendors who wanted payment. He had firms with whom he had lease agreements on equipment. He had been in his offices for twenty years, and had just renewed the lease for another five years with his now-anxious landlord. The business started to go downhill quickly. Clients and staff began leaving immediately. It took another seven months to negotiate a settlement with the landlord so that his wife or his estate did not have to pay the rest of the lease.

We had to find a buyer for the business, in what is called a death sale—one to sell immediately and at any price—and whatever value remained in the business had to be transferred as quickly as possible. But it took valuable time. His family only got about 20 percent of what the business should have been worth, and under the circumstances they were lucky to get that. It was just two weeks after his death that we handed it over to the new owner, but in that time it had lost 80 percent of its value, and all because of the chaos he'd inadvertently created by having no contingency plan. His family suffered through this, not knowing if they'd even be able to keep their home. Thank goodness we were able to uncover his insurance policies, so they came out of it with their home intact. Steve would have been horrified if he'd known all the chaos and loss that would result from his lack of planning for the people about whom he cared the most. But like so many of us do, he'd fooled himself into believing this could never happen to him.

This is the kind of risk that too many business owners out there are running today. They think they'll have time or there will be a happy ending. There isn't; happy endings are strictly for the movies. And the mess you leave when you have failed to plan properly for your own exit, anticipated or otherwise, is the mess your family and friends will be stuck with.

It shouldn't be that way. You've worked all these years. You've sacrificed, poured blood, sweat and tears in the business. You've created something of worth so that you can pass on to your heirs. But it's not going to have much worth if you don't run your exit plan as properly as you've run your business.

PLANNING DONE RIGHT

A good friend and longtime client, Karl, was an entrepreneurial physician who established a highly successful clinic about twenty-five years ago. A good deal of his wealth was tied up in it. As he was getting older, he decided he wanted to slow down. He wanted to protect his patients and his own team, sixty employees that counted on him, and he took that responsibility seriously.

He put together a succession plan, and part of that involved him approaching his partners first and asking them if they wanted to buy him out so that they could become the owners when he stepped down. Some were interested, but not enough of them, so he reached out to other medical institutions and groups and eventually found a great partner that came in to buy him out. He agreed to stay on for another few years to smooth the transition. Thanks to his smart planning, he got full value for the business, and he was able to diversify his own investment portfolio. He was able too to provide generously for his team, for his patients, his vendors, and, most importantly, for his family.

This whole book has been about mastering your cash flow, and building the value of your business. But if you fail to plan for your own exit from your enterprise, you're threatening the existence of all you've worked so hard to build. Don't put off this important step. If you don't want to do it, or can't find the time, think of the people that you're going to leave behind. It's not just your loved ones who will suffer—it's your

> *If you fail to plan for your own exit from your enterprise, you're threatening the existence of all you've worked so hard to build.*

team, people that have may have worked with you for many years. If the company falls apart, especially if these folks are in their fifties or sixties, the sudden loss of employment can have a devastating effect on their lives. Even if it's only for the sake of these others who depend on you, make sure that you've got your affairs in order, that you have a solid contingency plan and a succession plan in place, and that the people who need to have access to those documents know where they are to be found. Make sure your important papers aren't stuffed in a drawer somewhere that only you're aware of.

A good contingency plan is a lot like long term care insurance. While we certainly hope we're never called on to use it, having it is the responsible, smart thing to do. I've helped many business owners put together their contingency or succession plans, and I can tell you that having those in place offers tremendous peace of mind, just like a good insurance policy.

Chapter 12 Takeaways

- Failure to plan well for your own replacement in the event of your sudden disability or death leaves your enterprise in jeopardy, along with the people who count on you.

- Having a succession plan allows you to retire if you want to, while assuring a smooth transition of the business to the new management, to your partners, or to other people that you've grown within the company.

- The stronger the succession plan you have, the less risk you have for yourself, your loved ones, your team, and your clients or customers. It can also make you more attractive to potential investors or buyers.

- More important than a succession plan is, having a contingency plan in the event something happens suddenly to you.

- Having a contingency plan that outlines how the business will continue in your absence takes the weight of worry off everyone concerned.

- You've created something of worth so that you can pass on to your heirs. But it's not going to have much worth if you don't run your exit plan as properly as you've run your business.

Our Services

BOOK AL FOR YOUR NEXT EVENT!

Al is available for speaking engagements and would be an inspiring, motivating, and life-changing aspect of your next workshop, company event, or industry convention. All of his speeches are customized. He will work with you to understand your audience, your needs, and your goals to make your presentation a memorable one. He will work with you to create the perfect program for your audience.

Some keynote and workshop speaking topics include:

- How to Create the Life You Wish For Now and Forever!

- Finding More Cash in Everyday Business Decisions: Work Less in Life

- How to Work Less in Life and Still Live the Lifestyle You Want Now and Forever!

- Create a Championship Team of Experts: Why Poor Players Sentence You to Working Longer or Not Creating the Wealth You Could.

- The Wealth Building Formula®: How to Make the 100 Percent Correct Financial Decision All the Time

- Wealth, Humanity, and Changing the World: Why Good Wealth Management Is Not Just About the Dollars.

Al is also available for wealth management conversations. Learn more about him and follow him at www.AlZdenek.com. Also, feel free to take his personal and business assessments on his website to see if there is a way for you to find more cash flow in your life. He can also be followed on any of the following platforms:

www.linkedin.com/in/albertjzdenek/

@AlZdenek

www.facebook.com/albertjzdenek/

Start living the life you wish to lead *now* and in the future.